101 Treasurable Poems of Faith, Hope, and Love

Written By: Chad Joseph Thieman

Barb,

   I hope you enjoy the book. Thanks for always being there for Tina. I hope you come down and see us. God Bless!

Chad
Thieman

First published by Dog Ear Publishing
4010 W. 86th Street, Ste H
Indianapolis, IN 46268
www.dogearpublishing.net

ISBN: 978-160844-742-8

This book is printed on acid-free paper.

Printed in the United States of America

**His love is like a waterfall that flows
forever upon us. - Chad**

Psalm 42:7-8

In Loving Memory of my Grandma Boyd
...Who contributed so much love to my life.

A Special Thanks -

First and foremost, I would like to take this opportunity to thank the one who has truly been the inspiration behind all these poems, my Heavenly Father. I know He is within me and guides my writing. A special thanks goes out to my Lord Jesus Christ, who was sent by the Father that we might have life.

I would also like to personally thank my family, who have played such a major role in my life. Though they may not know it, they helped to inspire a lot of my poetry. Besides God and Christ, you were the greatest influences in my life, and I love you all so very much.

I would also like to thank my good friends, who have helped to inspire me either directly or indirectly; whether it has been through positive encouragement, sharing in an experience together, or investing in me and my work. Thank you for your support and friendship.

May God always be with each and every one of you.

Blessings, Chad

A Table of Contents

Chad Joseph Thieman

FOREWORD

I have had the privilege of knowing Chad Thieman for the past seven years. I have seen him grow in the knowledge of God through our Lord Jesus Christ, and I have witnessed his walk with God, in his integrity and honesty. He has been a great and loyal friend to me and to others in his life. He is inspiring in the things he does and the way he lives his life. He is a man who loves God, and wants truth in his walk with God and in his relationships with others. He lives a simple life, a life of simple faith but deep in thought of the things of God. His poems are simple, yet profound; easy to read, yet thought-provoking. One of my favorites is, *"The Drawbridge,"* a poem about God calling us to walk across the bridge into more of Him. Even in the midst of our pain and uncertainty, there's a drawbridge we can cross and be safe in His presence.

Let these simple poems speak to your heart, as they have mine. Let them draw you into a deeper walk with the Heavenly Father. It is my prayer that as you read these poems, inspired by the Spirit and written by this anointed psalmist that you will reflect upon, mull over, and pray over these words, and live out your faith with reverence and awe. May you be inspired by these, *101 Treasurable Poems of Faith, Hope, and Love.*

Jonathan Mull

Hickory, North Carolina

Introduction

The poetry in this book covers a wide range of topics from inspiration to romance, and from everyday life to religious themed poetry. There is something here for just about every audience. Since faith, hope, and love, all seem to fit well under the Christian subject heading, many have called it Christian poetry; however, when I write, I do so to express the way I feel at a certain time or to share a message of truth or inspiration, with those who need it the most. To me, this poetry is simply an expression of who I am and what I believe.

There are twenty poetry collections in this book, and they include 20 untitled excerpts, 101 poems, and 5 short stories. Some poems may appear twice, as they are categorized into two different collections of poetry. After each poem you will find a comment, dedication, or an inspirational verse I wrote, along with Bible chapter and verse numbers that relate to the poem. I laid this book out in such a way that it would promote the study of the scriptures. There are also proverbs and parables, as well as a bonus tribute section found at the end of the book. In all, this book includes close to 200 pieces of writing.

I believe these words that I have sent out, will accomplish everything that I am sending them out to accomplish. I pray that you will find inspiration throughout the pages of this book. May this poetry bring you a sense of peace and tranquility, and help you live a more beautiful and abundant life. I hope "101 Treasurable Poems of Faith, Hope, and Love," will be cherished by those who find wisdom and beauty, through the art of simplistic poetry.

—Chad

The Journey of Life Collection

Life is a journey that we must all take.
We all have decisions and choices to make,
And whichever the way that we choose to go,
We will find opportunities that help us to grow.

Acts 9:1-6

Followers of the Spirit

As Followers of the Spirit,
We know the direction in which to go,
And the route that we must take,
Down overgrown paths and narrow roads.
Because we follow close behind,
As God's Spirit leads throughout our lives.
Fully prepared are we,
For the obstacles that await.
Our leader has been here before;
He knows every little pathway,
And the traps that lay in store,
Along life's treacherous way.
We listen to that one still voice,
Keeping our mind's eye fully awake,
Submitting our lives to Him by choice.
We are guided by the Spirit that be,
And the Spirit of love must always lead,
Taking us places that we did not plan to go,
And showing us an abundant life,
That we did not previously know.

Dedicated to my friend, Curtis.

During his childhood, Curtis and his friends would play along a maze of paths between their houses. They knew the paths very well. They knew every one of them like the back of their hands and could find their way home in the dark. Curtis shared with me how Christ and the Holy Spirit operate in a similar manner. Our Lord has been here before, and He knows the obstacles and traps of the enemy. He sent the Holy Spirit to guide us along these paths of life and to help lead us home safely.

John 16:13

Chad Joseph Thieman

Highway to Heaven

When one road became two,
It was then, I had to decide,
The way in which I was to go,
Either the narrow or the wide.

The wide road had quite an appeal,
It seemed to be a downhill route,
But then the narrow one caught my eye,
And I began to have some doubt.

For though the wide road was traveled by many,
And the narrow one ascended Eagle's Bluff,
Still something in my spirit convinced me,
The low road for me just wasn't enough.

So I turned the wheel slightly to the right,
And gave my Chevy truck some gas.
I climbed up to those mountain heights,
For this scenic route, I could not pass.

I thought to myself, this is the better of the two,
And it may take me to some glorious place,
Whereas the other one, would not have such views,
And most likely have been just a waste.

The narrow road may be the more difficult of the two, but for the ones who travel this road, they find beauty and life even now.

Dedicated to Uncle Mike and Aunt Joyce.

Matthew 7:13-14

Life is a River

If life is a river,
We must swim upstream.
How hard it is,
But rewards it will bring.
We must go against the current,
And head for the source,
Keeping our heads above water,
And staying on course,
Leaving everything behind,
And not looking back,
We must strive for our goal,
Knowing how much we lack.
We can't follow the crowd,
That drifts right on by.
We must lift up our heads,
And look towards the sky.
Knowing God is here with us,
And helping us through.
The journey won't be easy,
But our dreams will come true.

Too many people today treat life as though it is going to take them somewhere. Many seem to forget that death awaits at the end of the line, like a vast waterfall spilling over great rocks. Believers know that they need to swim against the current and get back to the source. Those who have not trusted in the Lord will have their pride shattered, when they realize that they cannot save themselves.

Isaiah 25:11

Somewhere Down the Road

Somewhere down the road,
When I get to where I'm going,
I will reap what I've been sowing.
I will enter that city of gold.

I will forget these days of strife,
And partake of the Tree of Life.
I will throw off this heavy load,
Somewhere down the road.

Somewhere down the road,
When I walk upon the new Earth,
I will understand my true worth.
I will see what scriptures told.

I will lay beside the lion,
There will be no pain or cryin'.
I will walk the streets of gold,
Somewhere down the road.

Somewhere down the road,
When I get to where I'm heading,
I'll dance at the master's wedding,
At His banquet, I will be known.

I will find my heart's desires,
And my Father will lift me higher.
He will show me things untold,
Somewhere down the road.

Dedicated to all those who have worked along side me, at various banquet facilities. Remember, there is a great banquet awaiting those who believe, "Somewhere Down the Road."

Revelation 19:7-9

The Crossroads

She was a white rose
Without thorns.
It was such a blessing
The day she was born.
She was like an angel,
And she lived her life
Just that way.
She sang everywhere
She would go,
About meeting her Savior
At the crossroads.

Now it was a tragic loss
For this world,
The day God took away
That little girl.
But how could she have known
The ride in the church van
Would be her last?
It was time
For her to go,
And meet her Savior
At the crossroads.

    I will never forget where I heard the story that inspired this poem. I was up in Blowing Rock at an ice cream parlor, when I heard two ladies behind me talking about this little girl. I didn't catch her name or the correct title of the song she sang, but her story moved me so much, I had to write a poem about her.

Dedicated to the unknown girl in the story.

Hebrews 2:14-15

Chad Joseph Thieman

The Lord of Your Dance

It is the dawning of a new day,
So just forget your old ways.
You have been given another chance.
Ask Christ to lead and hold your hand,
And He will be the Lord of your dance.

So lay a rose on a forgotten grave.
Climb up a mountain just to pray.

Wake up early to watch the sunrise.
Wipe a teardrop from a little one's eyes.

Buy a sandwich for a homeless man.
Walk the beach to feel the sand.

Give a drink to the one who thirsts.
Be a blessing instead of a curse.

Take time in life to pause and reflect,
Try saying a prayer while you watch the sunset.

Always remember to laugh and to smile,
And look for the Father's love in the eyes of a child.

Serve the Lord and let it show.
Let your heart just overflow.
Trust in Christ and give Him a chance,
And let Him be the Lord of your dance.

Love is alive in those who believe and works through those who have faith.

Jeremiah 31:13

Walk with Me

Down a narrow path you lead,
Along the way, my soul you feed,
Sowing a most precious seed.
Walk with me Lord,
Walk with me.

Through the wood of evergreens,
Over the ridge, across the streams,
Longing for the pilgrim's dream.
Walk with me Lord,
Walk with me.

On the riverbank I pause to pray,
A ray of hope will show the way,
Through the storms of each new day.
Walk with me Lord,
Walk with me.

As I climb the rolling hills,
Passing fields that farmers till,
And the valley of the daffodil.
Walk with me Lord,
Walk with me.

During the day, a wonderful sight,
But when the day becomes night,
Then I'll need your guiding light.
Walk with me Lord,
Walk with me.

"Walk with Me" feels like a psalm from scripture. This simple poem carries with it an ambience of peace. It is a journey with the Creator, through His wonderful creation.

Dedicated to my step brother, Joe.

Luke 24:13-35

The Coastal Poetry Collection

There's a story that has remained untold,
About a purple clad pirate and a yellow marigold.
This treasure to him, was a gift from a young lad.
Discovering life's beauty therein,
The pirate gave up all that he had.

Dedicated to my brother, Curtis.

Matthew 13:44

A Lonely Vessel

Like a lonely vessel, I sail all alone,
Across this vast, empty ocean,
And back again,
To and fro I roam.

When there seems to be signs of life,
I will send the lifeboats out,
Only to find nothing at all in the end,
Except for fear and doubt.

This ocean is but a graveyard,
Of those glorious ships of the past.
Whatever happened to those ships,
Whatever happened? I dare to ask.

I looked forward to peace and tranquility,
After the storm had finally passed,
But now it seems to be me, by myself,
With no other vessels left.

Still I voyage out, across that peaceful calm,
With fervent expectation and hope,
That one day, I'll see on the distant horizon,
A line of sails from those grand ships arisin'.

We all have times, where we feel alone in our efforts. Sometimes we wonder if we should carry on. When you come upon times like these, I hope that you will remain determined and keep moving forward. I hope that you will continue to believe the impossible, for even these things are possible through God. This is a story of expectant hope, awaiting the return of the righteous ones, those fearless warriors of love.

1 Timothy 1:18-19

Angels in the Sand

As she sits beneath the warmth of a midday sun,
On the edge of this endless sea,
She watches her two daughters at play,
And it stirs up childhood memories.

As these thoughts start coming to mind,
She's taken back to another place in time,
Seeing three children laying face up in the sand,
With outstretched arms and waving their hands.

It was her brother, sister, and she,
Making sand angels down by the sea,
Moving their arms with a back and forth motion,
'Til three angels appeared, down by the ocean.

By time they had finished, a clear outline remained,
Until that high tide, in late evening came.
For her siblings and her, it was a fun game,
But looking back now, it was a bit lame.

She musters a smile and comes back to today,
Watching her two precious angels at play.

Dedicated to Michelle and her two precious angels.

One must become like a little child full of awe, love, and innocence; before they can ever hope to find lasting significance, in a world which has grown as cold as stone.

Matthew 18:2-5

A Seashell or an Oyster

If you were offered a seashell or an oyster,
Of which of these two would you choose?

Most would choose the seashell of course,
For it is the prettier one of the two.

Whether it has a smooth or rough surface,
Its beauty will surpass most always, it's true.

An oyster, on the other hand, many would pass by,
Because it is the more loathsome of the two.

Though if it were me, I think I would pick the oyster,
In hopes that a pearl might be hidden inside.

But if it were you, which one would you choose?
Or how would you decide?

True beauty lies hidden within, for the one who takes the time to seek and discover it.

Matthew 13:45-46

I am a Lighthouse

I am a lighthouse,
Standing faithful and true,
Set upon solid rock,
Shining my light upon you.

I am a lighthouse,
A beacon in darkest night.
My keeper, He never sleeps,
And my lamp burns ever bright.

I am a lighthouse,
My signal will pierce the storm,
Shining forth a guiding light,
To vessels lost and torn.

I am a lighthouse,
My lamp set high above the sea.
A guardian am I over vessels,
Who wander aimlessly.

The world cannot see God, unless they see Him through you. We are to be lighthouses, shining forth the light of Christ.

Dedicated to my friend, Stephanie.

Matthew 5:14-16
Philippians 2:15

Ode to the Lighthouse

There's a lamp in a tower
Out on the bay
Like a star over the bank
It shines like the day
Helping lost sailors
To find their way
Leading them home
Putting an end
To their tireless roam
Guiding them safely
Through the storm-filled night
A beacon over the harbor
Shining pure light

This poem is for all of those who feel lost at sea. Remember, there's a lighthouse that still shines gracefully.

John 8:12
John 12:44-46

Chad Joseph Thieman

Sandcastles

Seeking success, I devise my own plan,
Building a castle, with a foundation of sand.
I am a creator, I say in my heart,
Then a wave comes and tears my castle apart.

Each time I tell myself, *This time it will last*,
For many sandcastles have fallen in the past,
But still each night that tide rolls in,
And I have to begin building all over again.

My pride has blinded me from the truth.
I think there's something, I have to prove,
So I build a sandcastle again with my hands,
And admire the masterpiece created by man.

Every night the water comes to wash it away,
And I start all over again, on the very next day.
Ignoring humility and God's loving plan,
I keep building sandcastles, here in the sand.

I was inspired to write "Sandcastles," after I realized that seeking success apart from God, had led to many past failures.

Matthew 7:26-27

The Drawbridge

As I stand beside the troubled waters,
I feel a tugging in the depths of my heart.
I know I must reach the other side,
Yet in comfort, I wish not to part.

I can see a bridge in the distance,
A symbol of hope, calling out my name.
It's the bridge of good foundation,
Offering peace in the place of pain.

It opens up for stranded vessels,
And closes so men can cross,
Above the rushing water,
And the current's wicked toss.

It is Christ the mighty drawbridge,
And God's Spirit is drawing me,
Pulling at my heart and soul,
And helping me to see.

Showing me there's something more,
Awaiting there on the other side,
A place of love and goodness,
Without man's ignorance and pride.

God first inspired me to write "The Drawbridge," while I was waiting at one. I had to cross a drawbridge every day, to go to work on Wrightsville Beach.

Dedicated to my friend, Jonathan.

John 5:24

Chad Joseph Thieman

The Fisherman

An old man sat on a bench, clad in fisherman's attire.
His beard appeared ragged, and the wrinkles beneath his eyes seemed to sag.
In one hand he clutched an old, worn out fishing pole,
And the other, he moved about, while his stories were being told.

It seemed to be quite silly, for many times this scene, I did behold.
This fisherman was my father, and I thought him just crazy and old.
Every day he would walk out, to the end of Mercer's Pier,
Sitting down on a bench there, he would speak to all who would hear.

He told them tales of a young wise man, who once lived by the sea,
A man my father called master, for a following of fishermen had he.
Some people laughed at him and claimed he had lost his mind,
While others would draw near and listen, at least from time to time.

I tried to talk some sense into my dad and tried to keep him in,
But he'd say he had to leave and go fishing for some men.
One day I told him, "You are no fisherman, don't you see?
You've lost your mind and tell tall tales down by the sea."

But unbeknownst to me, that day would be the last of him, I'd see.
As he walked to the door, I saw a light in his eyes like never before.
He handed me a package, wrapped in brown paper and tied with twine,
And then he smiled at me and said, "My son, now it's your time."

After he left, I untied the twine and peeled the paper back carefully,
Revealing a Bible and a short message, asking me to read it please.
After reading several chapters, I stopped to answer the door,
That is when I learned, my dad drowned pulling a small child to shore.

That was thirty years ago, my friend, and I am quite different now.
You see I read that book my dad gave me, and I am sharing it with you now.
I learned the wise man is Christ, and to God he points the way.
My father, you see was out here, changing hearts each and every day.

Now I'm the old man who sits on this bench, in this old fishing attire.
My beard appears ragged, and the wrinkles beneath my eyes seem to sag.
In one hand I clutch my father's old worn out fishing pole,
And my other hand, I move about, while my stories are being told.

I speak of a young wise man, who once lived by the sea,
A man I now call master, for a following of fishermen had he.
Sure some laugh at me and claim I've lost my mind,
But others will draw near and listen, at least from time to time.

"The Fisherman," is a fictional piece I wrote that carries with it, a lot of inspiration. I included the name of a popular pier at Wrightsville Beach, within the poem.

Dedicated to Cherry and the boys at "Fishers of Men."

Mark 1:17

The Lord is my Captain

My tattered vessel was in the storm,
My ship was lost at sea.
In the wind my sail was torn.
The Lord, seeing my boat was worn,
Reached out to rescue me.

Though the storm was mighty strong,
He simply raised his hands up high,
Commanding for the waves to calm,
And the storm winds to subside.

Now the Lord is my captain,
And He fixed the boat just right.
On the journey much will happen,
But I know those sails are flappin',
So I'll just sit back and enjoy the ride!

This poem shows the freedom and peace that can be found, when Christ is in control. He calms the storms and offers rest for the weary.

Matthew 11:28
Mark 4:37-41

The Sea of Serenity

The Sea of Serenity,
I hear it calling out to me.
Through the calmness of my soul,
I feel your tender Spirit flow.

I hear the whisper of your waters,
As they move me, by and by,
Like a vessel upon the ocean,
Or the eagle that takes to fly.

I long to feel the moving wind,
That brings these waves, back again,
To move this vessel, through and through,
Bringing me, another glimpse of you.

Your shimmering waters, sustain me,
Beneath the bright and risen sun.
They're telling me, my journey here,
Has only just begun.

I'm floating as the tender reed,
Always seeking the Spirit that be.
I yearn to sail this uncharted sea,
The sea, they call, Serenity.

All possessions, I have left behind,
In exchange for this wind in my sail.
I explore your waters, hoping to find,
My life, my legacy, a treasurable tale.

But when this journey is complete,
And my body lies down to sleep,
No more sorrow, shall I see,
Only the calmness, of Serenity.

Forever, I will drink of your deep,
The waters stir and I am set free.
When this vessel, you no longer see,
Know that I am one, with Serenity.

Dedicated to Dale, in his loving memory and to his surviving family, Rosalie, Samantha, Ashley, and Eric.

John 4:14

Chad Joseph Thieman

Wedding on the Beach

(Original Version)

Barefoot on the beach they stand,
Two lovers hand in hand,
Looking intently into each others eyes,
Sharing their vows beneath a blue sky.

Each of them speaking words from the heart,
Making the promise, until death not to part.

A bond of love is being formed this day,
As these two bodies become as one,
On the edge of this seemingly endless sea,
Beneath the rays of a midday sun.

God, family, and friends are witnesses here,
Beholding this beautiful sight,
As these two souls join together in love,
And two hearts begin to unite.

They place their wedding bands,
Upon each others hands;
It's a beautiful sight to be seen.
Their love is forever represented here,
By these two encircling rings.

A reminder of the true circle of love,
Man, his wife, and God above.

Let them never forget this holy bond,
And Heavenly Father, remind them always,
To seek your love from beyond.

And now as they move forward from here,
Lord, I pray you will bless all of their plans,
As they leave behind this cherished moment in time,
And their two sets of footprints in the sand.

I wrote "Wedding on the Beach," for my dad's wedding. This is the original version. I wrote an alternate version which is also included in this book, since the wedding took place in a gazebo, overlooking Kure Beach.

Dedicated to my dad and Kathy, who were married at Fort Fisher.

Mark 10:7-9

The Romance Collection

The dawn is breaking...
My love, she's waiting...
Her arms embracing...
As wind embraces the tree,
Her love has set me free.

I believe that desire and romance can build and be stronger in those who wait for the right person. When it does happen, it will be all the more beautiful. I have witnessed this type of love on a few occasions, and I would rather wait to experience that kind of love and beauty.

Song of Solomon 7:12-13

A Mystical Honeymoon

We walk the shore of a foreign land,
With tender strides across the sand,
Holding each other close with gentle hands,
You are my princess, and I am your man.

Like a slow dance in the moonlit night,
Our bodies sway beneath soft, cascading light.
Like dancing stars, in our own right,
The heavens look down, beholding the sight.

I pull you closer and move the hair from your face,
And lay you down gently, with tender embrace.
One hand glides slowly, untying your lace,
As we begin making love, in this mystical place.

I hope this poem will take the reader to that mystical place, where love abides.

Song of Solomon 8:3

Chad Joseph Thieman

A Rose Every Day

I give my love a rose every day,
Hand picked from the rose bushes,
I planted last May.

She's what makes my days so special,
And no one day is better than the next.

Every morning she will awaken to find,
A freshly cut, red rose from the vine,
In a glass vase, upon our old, oak chest.

Dedicated to my three favorite Roses.

Song of Solomon 6:2

A Rose in a Box

A small wooden box,
With the scent of fresh cedar,
Would contain my gift,
To show her I need her.

A crimson red rose,
In this box made for Ashtons.
I laid it down gently,
Upon a cushion of satin.

This gift for my sweetheart,
On satin inlay,
Would be the perfect gift,
For our special day.

After opening the box,
She lit up with a grin.
This rose in a box,
It touched her within.

A memory to cherish,
This gift that I gave,
And my love for her there,
So adamantly displayed.

"A Rose in a Box," makes for a special gift. Sometimes it's the smallest gifts that leave the greatest impressions. The inspiration for this poem, came from a gift my stepfather gave my mother.

Dedicated to my mother and Ken.

Song of Solomon 2:1

Chad Joseph Thieman

Love's Sonata

With my heart you must be gentle,
Soft as light, emitted from the candle.
Too many times, I have been hurt before.
Too many times, I've been forlorn.

With you, I feel complete, my love.
Your soft breath dances upon my cheek.
Long forgotten are those yesterdays of infamy.
Our love, tonight, feels like a symphony.

As the universe joins in the melody,
Our bodies become one entirely.
Our souls give reciprocal affection,
While our flesh comes together with intimate attraction.

My skin touching yours and yours returning the favor,
Upon the wall our shadows dance, in silhouettes,
While we enjoy love's flavor, and savor it.

"Love's Sonata," is a reminder that true intimacy is beautiful and was designed by God. It is the coming together of two people as one flesh. This is why the marriage bed should be kept pure.

Song of Solomon 1:1-4
Mark 10:6-8

Message in a Bottle

A message to my love I sent,
A poem with the sweetest words.
I told of the longing in my heart,
And the love imprisoned there from the start.

Then I rolled it up and stuffed it in,
A small glass bottle empty of gin.
I took the bottle, with my message in there,
Down to the riverbank where time laid bare.

I prayed this message, God would give her,
And threw it in that lonely river.
I thought, one day my love will find,
That bottle empty of gin,
And upon opening it up,
Discover my love there within.

This poem is one of my favorites. It's a poem about a simple man seeking to find the love that he has forever longed for, the love that would make his life complete.

Romans 8:24-25

My Love is in Her Garden

My love is in her garden,
Blond hair streaming from her head.
She sits amidst flowering milkweed,
Beneath monarchs of gold and red.

Her gown is ever flowing,
A dress of Alice blue,
As she runs her fingers slowly,
Across the grass and morning dew.

Her beauty far surpasses,
All that I could ever dream.
Such tenderness and gentle love,
Are rarely ever seen.

She comes here quite often now,
To sit, reflect, and pray,
And when she starts to sing,
The doves come out to play.

The sun always turns its gaze,
To perceive this beauty below.
Its rays shine forth with softest light,
Upon her beautiful soul.

My love is in her garden,
And I have missed her mirth,
So I have come out to my love,
To sit and laugh with her.

A loving woman is a beautiful woman, and her beauty will never cease with age.

Song of Solomon 4:10-16
Isaiah 51:3

The Helpless Romantic

I want to see your soft body in the moonlight,
And dance with you in the pouring rain,
Lay with you beneath a starry night sky,
Say I love you and whisper your name.

I want to ride horses across the countryside,
And walk with you barefoot in the stream,
Have a glass of wine and watch the ocean tide,
And relive it all over again in my dreams.

I want to see the sunlight dancing in your hair,
And go mountain climbing with you at my side,
Sit on top and watch the sunset from there,
And fall asleep beneath that Carolina sky.

I want to kiss you in a lighthouse tower,
And bathe with you in a mountain stream.
I want to lay with you in a field of wildflowers,
And relive it all over again in my dreams.

You will never find the love of your dreams, unless you first plant the seed of love and help someone become the one your dreaming of. The most beautiful and perfect flower could not exist, until someone took the time to plant it.

Song of Solomon 2: 10-13

The Life Lessons Collection

If the Maker gives me my fullness of days,
And in health lets me tarry,
Then not one of them shall be stolen away,
Lest in knowledge of it, many grow wary.

Job 14:5

Brittle Bits of Thought

So delicate are the memories,
To the one advanced in age,
So fragile to the point of breakage,
Like a feeble antique vase,
Or a dainty piece of china,
Starting to show its age,
Like a worn out and easy to rip page,
About to fall out from their life story,
These memories of younger days of glory.
These thoughts, like glass now seem to shatter,
Those thoughts, to them that seemed to matter,
Leaving behind little fragments,
That must be gathered up bit by bit,
While the elderly one stops and ponders,
In a quiet place they sit,
An attempt to put together,
Those brittle bits of thought,
And recall those cherished moments,
And the comfort that they brought.

Dedicated to Stella, who passed after a long struggle with Alzheimer's disease.

1 Timothy 5:1-2

Chad Joseph Thieman

Canary on the Bough

Once I had a yellow canary,
And I loved that bird so.
He sang the most beautiful song,
And was colored in vibrant gold.

But when I left the house one day,
I forgot to latch the door of the cage,
And upon returning there again,
I found the cage empty,
With no canary within.

Where he flew, I did not know,
Until I saw his bright yellow glow,
As he sat upon the windowsill,
And though one moment there,
The next he had left it bare.

So I went to the window,
To get a closer look.
I watched as he flew down,
Past the old mill, near the brook.

So I sprinted outside as fast as I could,
Down to the mill, the brook, and the wood.
When I arrived, I saw the canary sitting there,
On an old maple branch, which showed its wear.

But still I couldn't catch the canary,
For he flew from bough to bough,
And where he is today, I do not know.
On occasion, I find him singing there though,
Upon that old and weathered maple bough.

This poem is a good representation of freedom. As believers we find our freedom in Christ, no longer are we slaves to sin. We are now free to sing our beautiful song, with love and thanksgiving.

Psalms 104:12
Galatians 5:1

Finding Success

I failed many times,
But never the same.
I tried many things,
All too often in vain.

I walked many a road,
Seeing where they might go,
Finding myself lost,
Or the people there false.

Indeed it is true,
You learn the most,
When you lose,
Albeit, what not to do.

The ones who succeed,
Learn how to lead,
And surround themselves,
With those who believe.

All failures are tests,
Along the road to success,
But you'll find it true,
If the Father be in you.

*Those who trust God and are willing to risk failure over and over again,
greatly increase their chances of figuring out how to succeed.*

Proverbs 3:5-6

Chad Joseph Thieman

If There Were No Tomorrow

If there were no tomorrow,
How would you live out today?
Would you live it with happiness,
Or dwell in the sorrow?
If today was the last,
And there were no tomorrow.

Would you show those you love,
Just how much you do care?
Take your son to a ball game,
Or your daughter, to the fair?

Would you climb a lofty mountain,
And take time to enjoy the view?
Would you hand out forgiveness,
To all those, who have wronged you?

If there were no tomorrow,
How would you live out today?
Would you live it with happiness,
Or dwell in the sorrow?
If today was the last,
And there were no tomorrow.

Would you take time to pray?
If so, then what would you say?
Would you thank God for every moment,
And make the most of this day?

Would you stop and smell the roses,
Or go fishing with an old friend?
Would you write a beautiful poem,
And tell someone that you love them?

If there were no tomorrow,
How would you live out today?
Would you live it with happiness,
Or dwell in the sorrow?
If today was the last,
And there were no tomorrow.

Life would be so much more beautiful, if we lived each day as though it were our last.

Dedicated to John, Kathy, Philip, and Daphne

James 4:13-14
Luke 12:16-21

Chad Joseph Thieman

Like the Shepherd

A good father is like a shepherd,
Who leads his children like young lambs.
He guides them day by day,
Teaching them all the Lord's ways.

Blessed is the father who does these things,
For to his children, great love he brings.

He guides them with his staff and rod of correction,
And steers his children in the right direction,
Fulfilling their physical, emotional, and spiritual needs,
Training them how to survive and succeed.

A father is a physical representation,
Of our spiritual Father up in Heaven.
So always honor your father's position,
And remember it's ordained,
A God given mission.

Dedicated to my father.

A father disciplines his children. Those who belong to the Heavenly Father are disciplined by Him. He does not discipline those who are not His own. In this way we know that we are children and well loved, if the Father is strict with us when we stray.

Proverbs 13:24, Ephesians 6:4, Hebrews 12:5-7

Raspberry-Pickin'

If I hold on to, a single regret,
It may very well be,
Passing up raspberry pickin',
Just grandma and me.

How I now wish,
I could turn back the hands of time,
And spend an afternoon with grandma,
Picking raspberries from the vine.

She said it would be but an hour,
And I might enjoy the simple pleasure,
Of a late spring-time pickin',
In perfect sunny weather.

But for one reason or another,
I opted to stay back,
And now I wish I hadn't.

What was so important,
That it was worth missing,
An afternoon with my grandma,
Raspberry-pickin'?

Dedicated to my great grandmother.

Psalm 92:14-15

Reflections

Reflections are seen in the mirror when we awake.
You can behold them in windows or out on the lake.
At night you see a reflection of this life it seems,
In your imagination while you sleep and you dream.

Always remember it's just an image of what is true,
For it is by your reflection that this world judges you.
What they see on the outside, they think is within.
It is the eye of the flesh that leads many to sin.

But God sees more than just a reflection of you.
God can see your heart, and He knows what is true.
If you look in the mirror and don't like what you see,
Remind yourself and say, "God's Spirit is in me."

The fool looks only at the outward appearance, the wise man looks for the beauty within.

1 Corinthians 13:12

The Story of the Crosses

One night a man was walking alone in the city. The man had many worries on his mind and could not find comfort. While he was walking he noticed a stranger sitting on a curb beneath a streetlight. The stranger could tell that the man was troubled, so he asked him if he believed in God. "I have never seen any sign of God in this city," the man replied.

The stranger pointed up and told the man to look a little closer. "Notice how all the power that gives light to the city, hang on these wooden crosses". The stranger continued, "Think of Christ as your power line. He also hung on a wooden cross and gives power and light to the world. Without the Lord's sacrifice all men would live in darkness. The Father knew this and sent us His only begotten Son that through Him the true light could come into our lives." The stranger smiled at the man and said, "As you can see, God still leaves reminders of His Son everywhere."

The man thanked the stranger and started to walk away. He had only taken a few steps, when he turned back to find that the stranger was gone. The man gave thanks to God and headed home counting the crosses.

I remember driving down the road one day and taking notice of the many crosses that lined the street. I noticed how the power lines carried the light to the city. I really felt like God laid it on my heart, to write this story. I wrote "The Story of the Crosses," about fifteen years ago, and it was the very first inspirational piece that I had ever written. It is my hope that this story will be remembered and retold for many years to come. The next time you are driving down the street, I hope you will take time to notice these crosses, and remember the sacrifice that Christ made for us all. He died, so we could have eternal life.

Dedicated to my friends at St. Francis, in Lenoir, NC.

1 Corinthians 1:18

Chad Joseph Thieman

The Angel Collection

A starving girl is on the television set,
You can see the hunger in her eyes.
Is she just someone else's problem,
Or is she an angel in disguise?

Hebrews 13:1-3

Angels In The Sand

As she sits beneath the warmth of a midday sun,
On the edge of this endless sea,
She watches her two daughters at play,
And it stirs up childhood memories.

As these thoughts start coming to mind,
She's taken back to another place in time,
Seeing three children laying face up in the sand,
With outstretched arms and waving their hands.

It was her brother, sister, and she,
Making sand angels down by the sea,
Moving their arms with a back and forth motion,
As three angels appeared down by the ocean.

By time they had finished, a clear outline remained,
Until that high tide, in late evening came.
For her siblings and her, it was a fun game,
But looking back now, it was a bit lame.

She musters a smile and comes back to today,
Watching her two precious angels at play.

Dedicated to Carole and her two precious angels.

The Kingdom of Heaven is developing right here on earth. You just need to have the eyes of a child, to see it taking shape all around you.

Mark 10:14

Like an Angel With Broken Wings

She roams through this life looking for worth.
Being blessed with beauty that is her curse.

The other girls talk and give her bad looks.
Their jealousy stings and God knows she hurts.

She made some mistakes that weigh on her mind,
Now she no longer thinks she has what it takes.
She dreams her dreams but then she awakes,
Finding herself alone.

Just like an angel with broken wings,
God placed her here on this earth,
To sing her song through suffering,
Unaware of tomorrow and what it might bring.

She wants to fly but can't leave the ground.
She looks for love but it's nowhere to be found.
All she finds is empty promises.

Until finally one day, love breaks through,
Like a ray of sun, piercing thick fog.
She remembers what she was put here to do,
And begins singing her new song.

Now she's catching dreams like butterflies,
Spreading her wings, she readies to fly,
When love swoops down like a breath of fresh air,
And lifts her up to God knows where,

Like a feather rising high above,
Sailing on a prayer, a wind of gentle love.
Drifting as a white cloud in the dreamer's sky,
To a place of peace, where poets never cry.

She draws near to the angels,
To meet her bridegroom in the air.
She lived a life of faithfulness,
While others didn't care.

She once was a damsel in distress,
Imprisoned on this earth,
But love broke through,
And came down to rescue her.

This poem has a much deeper meaning, hidden within it. It is a picture of the persecuted church. The church is represented here as a young woman redeemed by the love of her bridegroom, who is Christ Jesus.

1 Thessalonians 4:17

Chad Joseph Thieman

Mothers are Angels in Disguise

Some take their mothers for granted,
They seem ordinary in their eyes.
But if they would look a little bit deeper,
They would be in for a real surprise.

You see a mother's love is our protection.
She hides us safely in her arms,
Guiding us in God's direction,
With discipline and firm correction.

Yet most cannot see this it seems,
They are looking with earthly eyes,
Blinded to all those spiritual things.

Therefore the gift of a mother is for the wise,
And those who can understand God's blessings.
For these look through with spiritual eyes,
To see God's angel beneath her disguise,
And understand the great love that she brings.

This is a poem that really needed to be written. Mothers are such a gift from God, yet most in today's generation have lost respect for their mothers. They have not seen or understood the gift of a mother. I hope that you can relate to this analogy above, when thinking of your mother.

Dedicated to my loving mother.

1 Samuel 2:18-21

My Guardian Angels

I have angels up in Heaven,
Twenty-four/seven,
Looking upon my Father there,
Covering me with fervent prayer.

He commands them concerning me,
Wherever it is that I may be,
To guard me in all my ways,
Each and every single day.

These loyal servants from up above,
Spiritual guardians of His love.
Sometimes I feel them touching my skin,
A reminder for me to refrain from sin.

A few times I've heard their ancient hymns,
While resting late at night,
And once I believe I saw one,
Appear and come to light.

These angels, they watch over me.
I wouldn't want to go without,
My ever faithful guardian angels,
Their existence I do not doubt.

I always know when they draw near,
For they dissolve that spirit of fear,
And surround me with the Spirit of love,
My guardian angels from above.

Many of the lines in this poem were taken from verses found throughout Scripture. I think we would be shocked if we had the spiritual sight to see these angels working around and among us. I can vaguely remember one story in Scripture, where a man was given such sight. As he looked out, he saw a vast army of angelic beings that were on the side of Israel.

Dedicated to my friend, Jamie.

2 Kings 6:15-18
Matthew 18:10

Chad Joseph Thieman

The Angels and the Quilt

I witnessed last night,
In a vision, in a dream,
Four tiny angels,
Knitting it seemed.

All looking quite busy,
And taking great care,
Weaving together phrases,
And words in the air.

I saw scissors and needles,
And thimbles and thread,
As I lay below watching,
From my hospital bed.

They snipped and they sewed.
Their needlework was fine.
They showed no signs of slowing,
And the words they all entwined.

The angels worked diligently,
And they whispered all the while,
Until they had finally finished,
And one said with a smile...

This quilt was made with love,
It was sewn with great care,
From all who have kept you,
In thoughts and in prayers.

Every prayer that they prayed,
Formed a thread, it is true,
And we wove them together,
As a reminder for you.

The words are for comfort,
Warmth and healing they'll bring.
Then the angels were gone,
And I awoke from the dream.

I noticed when I woke up,
A blanket covering me.
I wondered if somehow,
This was more than a dream.

Dedicated to Junior.

    This poem was based on a true experience. My grandfather's brother had this vision while he was in the hospital. There was even an article published on his experience.

Psalm 91:10-11

The Visitation

There once was a man who had a grand vision. In his vision, an angel appeared and took him away. First, he was shown the Kingdom of Heaven. There he saw the rewards of those who had lived righteously. He also saw many seated with Christ on His throne and others walking the streets of gold. The man asked the angel, "How have these earned such a reward?"

The angel then told the man, "These sowed the good seed and are reaping life. The seeds they planted, were seeds of love, joy, peace, patience, kindness, goodness, faithfulness, gentleness, and self-control. They loved and feared the Lord, and repented of all wrongdoing. Everyone here has been given blessings according to their faith and good works."

The angel explained by using a parable of a farmer sowing seed in his field, "If the farmer sows little, then he receives little; if the farmer sows much, then he receives an abundance. Also, if a farmer sows good seed in his field, then he will reap a good harvest; but if a farmer sows bad seed, then he will reap a bad crop."

After explaining this, the angel took the man to a vast lake of fire, and the man saw many wailing and being led into the fire. The man asked the angel, "How have these come to deserve such a fate as this?"

The angel replied, "These are those who practiced sorcery, fornication, and murder. These are the cheaters, liars, thieves, and adulterers. Their fleshy desires they fulfilled continually without repentance, and they have destroyed many because of their lifestyles. The seeds they planted have now become a great harvest and they are partaking of it, reaping all that they have sown. Instead of leading people to life, they have brought them into this fire along with them. These did not fear the Lord, and they loved not His commandments. Though the seeds seemed small to these people, they grew, and produced a great harvest of death. You see, the choice of life or death was laid out before all men."

Then the man heard those being led into the fire, repenting to the Lord, and a voice came down from Heaven saying, "Are you repenting now, after the time for repentance is over?"

The people were crying to the Lord, "We were warned of this fire but we did not believe. Oh, Lord your judgments are righteous and just!"

Every one of them suffered in the fire, according to the sins they had committed.

This story is a reminder that whatever we sow, we will one day have to reap. My brethren, seek the Heavenly Father that you may plant only good seed. If you stray from Him, return to the Father and repent of all your sin, with fasting and mourning, fear and trembling. Our God is not only a God of justice but equally a God of mercy. His love lifts up the broken-hearted. He is slow to anger, holding off His judgments and wrath that we may all receive and partake freely of His forgiveness, mercy, and love. All these blessings we find through our Lord Jesus Christ.

Luke 13:1-9, Luke 16:19-31, Mark 9:43

Chad Joseph Thieman

Unwanted and Unloved

Never to see the light of day,
A little angel whisked away.

Unwanted and unloved,
Upon this earthly land.
Enter into Heaven's love,
And let Jesus hold your hand.

So still your lifeless body lay,
Oh, little angel whisked away.

Unwanted and unloved,
Upon this earthly land.
Enter into Heaven's love,
And let Jesus hold your hand.

What is there left to say,
A little angel was whisked away.

Unwanted and unloved,
Destroyed by human hands.
Fly like the morning dove,
To fulfill God's greater plan.

If the heart is pumping blood, there is life flowing within. The life is in the blood, and life should be considered sacred by all men.

Dedicated to Aunt Mary Jo and Uncle Ron.

Psalm 139:13-16
Proverbs 24:11-12

The Craftsman Collection

He dips His brush with oranges, yellows, and reds,
Painting in autumn, the canopies of leaves overhead.

He colors the evening sky with pink and purple hues,
And during the day, He adds blotches of white,
Upon His canvas of deep blue.

Romans 1:20

A Cracked Pot

How cracked this pot once was,
That it could hold no water within,
Placed upon the shelf of life,
Burdened with emptiness and sin.

Forgetting the hand that once shaped it,
And left alone here to rot,
Until the day it remembered who made it,
And desired to become a useful pot.

The Potter felt sad for this vessel He made,
And forgave it of all of its sin.
He patched it up with love and mercy,
And sat it upon that shelf once again.

This time, though, for daily use,
To fulfill His wonderful plan.
He filled it up with living water,
This simple vessel of man.

Now I'm filled with the Spirit of love,
All the way up to the brim,
For I surrendered myself to the Potter,
And live my life out for Him.

I once was a vessel that brought dishonor,
Sitting broken on the shelf of life,
But now things are different, you see,
I bring the Potter honor and delight.

If you feel like a broken or cracked pot, maybe it is time that you put your trust in the one who created you. Seek healing, forgiveness, and restoration in the Potter's hands.

Jeremiah 18:1-10

Chad Joseph Thieman

A Painter of Light

As an inspired poet, I help create a masterpiece,
Using living words filled with light.
Believing my work will never fade away,
I invest my time, my talent and my life.

Like the painter, I have my canvas,
All those sad and lonely hearts.
This is where I paint the light,
And hope to leave my mark.

Simple poems are easily forgotten, I know,
If the readers aren't moved deep within.
So I paint these words with soft strokes and delicacy,
And let the Spirit of love guide my pen.

Though I may never have these poems displayed,
Framed nicely and hung in some museum,
I will continue to paint the light,
And with my brush spread love and freedom.

My hope is to be a poet of light, and if these words come alive within you, then you know that my legacy is true.

Psalm 119:130

The Potter's Wheel

Our Father is a Potter, spinning His clay,
Creating some vessels of honor and others of disdain.
By pushing the peddle down with his heel,
He wrought each vessel upon spinning wheel.

The Potter shapes each one however He feels,
Upon that old revolving Potter's wheel.

What is the clay that it may suggest,
How it be made, shaped, or wrest?
The Potter shapes each vessel as He sees fit,
Whether it be made for wrath or for righteousness.

He molds each one of us through pleasure and pain.
Whether it be through good times or bad,
The honorable vessels will always gain,
And those of dishonor in blindness remain.

When life seems to spin out of control,
Just remember that Potter's wheel below,
And know His hands are guiding the clay,
As he tears, smooths, and shapes us every day.

Surrender your life and no longer resist,
And you will see the abundant life you have missed.
Submit to the Potter, and He will create a vessel of luster,
One made in His image, for true righteousness.

*Surely the one who made us, knows how to reshape us. Surrender
yourself to the Potter, and He will make you an honorable vessel.*

Romans 9

Chad Joseph Thieman

The Goldsmith's Shop

I walked down the village road,
Until I came to a stop,
In front of a old, rustic looking building,
With a sign that read, *The Goldsmith's shop*.

Upon entering in,
Through a large wooden door,
I met a man with a grin,
Halfway across the floor.

Beside a furnace we stood,
Surrounded by ashes,
The craftsman and me,
And he adjusted his glasses.

He showed me how to hammer and chisel,
And we tested the gold in the fire,
Working we removed all the impurities.
Though I grew weary, he never tired.

It was my first day as the new apprentice,
And looking back now, I was so anxious.
I wanted to develop that craftsman's skill,
And join up with the rest in his guild.

But patience was the first lesson taught.
It took me nearly two weeks of time,
Until a vessel of luster I had wrought,
A polished vessel of gold so fine.

I ponder how the days have flown by.
I'm watching my life flash before my eyes.
You see, I have finally come to my end,
And soon I will meet the true Craftsman.

Once I was like an imperfect, gold rock,
But a sacrifice was made, and I have been bought.
Through the Father's mercy, patience, and love,
This vessel of luster was wrought from above.

Now, as I walk that street of pure gold,
I come to a stop,
Beneath a sign that reads,
The Goldsmith's Shop.

For the child of God, everything works together for their own good. So find joy in your suffering, for it is always beneficial in the shaping of your character. No father wants to see his children suffer. You are like gold, being tested in fire. All things are working together for your benefit, though you may not be able to currently see it. God will not let any of His children remain in their current state of sin. He will take away all your impurities, leaving behind only the finest and purest gold.

Zechariah 13:7-9

The Faith Collection

Shine down upon me,
Oh, Light of the World.
Plant a treasure within,
Like that of a precious pearl.

John 8:12

A Step of Faith

Though the way seems dark and dreary,
Though the body is worn and weary,
Step out in faith, and trust in Christ.
Step out in faith, and don't think twice.
Invite God's Spirit to come inside,
And step out in faith, to let it guide.

Another opportunity awaits to be found,
But fear has a way of keeping us down.
Step out in faith, and trust in Christ.
Step out in faith, and don't think twice.
Beyond the shadow of doubt you'll see,
A step of faith, will set you free.

Dedicated to Leo, for his courage and faith along the path to recovery.

Psalm 119:133

Chad Joseph Thieman

Faith Moves Mountains

Some people see faith as a belief,
Others see it as God's great relief.
I see faith as knowing what is true,
Even when mountains obstruct my view.

From my experience faith always delivers.
Faith can part the mightiest river.
It can be gentle as footprints in the sand,
Or it can lift mountains high above land,
And cast them into the sea afar.
Faith can take us beyond the highest star.

Faith can move great mounds of earth,
Or be felt by a child, who sees a mother's worth,
And even when fear tries hard to block and hide,
Faith will appear to push those mountains aside.

For too long we have let this giant sleep,
But if this sleeping giant was to awake,
The very foundations of earth would shake,
And every mountain would move from its place,
For the greatest power is that of faith.

Dedicated to my uncle Joe and aunt Jan.

If you have faith the size of a single grain of sand, you'll be able to accomplish your greatest goals and plans.

Mark 11:23

Faith Versus Fear

Fear is a thick cloud,
Hiding God's holy truth.
Faith is knowing full well,
When you can't see the proof.

Fear holds you back,
So you'll give up the dream.
Faith pushes you forward,
Beyond your mortal means.

Fear puts you in a box,
Keeping you from living life.
Faith breaks through the walls,
Cutting fear like a knife.

Fear is a dark shadow,
Trying hard to block the light,
Leading many to anger,
Hatred, suffering, and strife.

But faith is a beacon of hope,
Love, and everlasting life.
So let's walk by our faith,
And not just our sight.

Many fears must die, before faith can be made alive within you. Fear only God that you obey His commands, and all your other fears will dissolve, as your faith grows in Him.

Psalm 91:5-8
2 Corinthians 5:7

Chad Joseph Thieman

Falling Again

There I go, falling again,
Another obstacle around the bend,
Leading me off the narrow path.
Father, I wonder where you are at,
When I start falling again.

When I question you about this,
Your answer always amazes me.
You simply say, "My child,
You can't stumble on your knees."

So I get down on my knees,
As humble as I can.
I ask you Father please,
Forgive me for falling once again.

*For the answers to life, this is the key: when you are lost, remember
me.*

1 John 1:9

God's Warrior

Go forth God's warrior,
Strong and fierce.
The face of darkness,
Thy light shall pierce.

In thy heart, eternal life.
In thy mind, renewed sight.

Upon thy head, for your protection,
Put on the helmet of salvation.

Around thy thigh, the belt of truth,
Trusting God for His reproof.

Over thy shoulders, cover your chest,
With the breastplate of righteousness.

Down below, upon thy feet,
Strap the sandals of God's true peace.

At thy side, the shield of faith,
Keep it close throughout your days.

In thy hand, for all to fear it,
Lift high the sword of God's own Spirit.

Go forth God's warrior,
Strong and fierce.
The face of darkness,
Thy light shall pierce.

Those who think with their heads rationalize things and can be consumed with fear and doubt. Those who think with their hearts, are less concerned with possible outcomes and more likely to become fearless warriors of God. Let the Word of God be your sword, and let His love be the banner flying overhead.

Dedicated to my friend, Chance.

Ephesians 6:10-18
1 Timothy 6:12

Chad Joseph Thieman

Possess Me

Heavenly Father,

Possess me with your loving Spirit,
So that I may live like Christ.
Help me put my ways to death,
So that I can find true life.

Fill me up with who you are,
Yes, come and live within,
So I may be perfect like you,
Without the stain of sin.

Possess me with the Spirit of Christ,
And show me all that is true.
Rid me of my fleshy nature,
Father, I belong to you.

Give me of your Spirit nature,
So loving, gentle, and meek.
The world will always oppose it,
But in you, I will find my peace.

Possess me with the Spirit of love,
No longer will I live for the flesh.
The flesh seeks only to please itself,
But the Spirit seeks righteousness.

So enter into this temple you made.
Let your Spirit descend like a dove.
For I am your prize possession,
And you my God are love.

Possess me with your loving Spirit,
For this is where wisdom starts.
Teach me that your law is love,
And write it upon my heart.

Give me courage and strength today,
So that I may follow your call.
Help me spread the Gospel to others,
For you will become all in all.

Possess me with the Spirit of Christ,
For in Him, I am forgiven.
Father, help me live my life for you,
And let love be my only religion.

I wrote "Possess Me," as a prayer. I wanted people to understand that true religion is not following the traditions of men. True religion is simply letting God live within you and letting Him work through you. Our bodies were created as temples, and we are now called to be born of His Spirit. As sons of God in Christ, we partake of His spiritual nature, just as Christ took on our fleshy nature. A spirit born of God can neither sin nor die but finds oneness in the very essence of Christ.

Ephesians 1:13-14

Chad Joseph Thieman

The Hope Collection

Beneath a canopy of leaves,
A small olive branch sways in the breeze.
She's a symbol of hope and peace,
Amidst the war, hate, and disease.

Dedicated to Olivia and her mother, Stephanie.

Isaiah 17:5-7

Hope Floats

Hope is something wished for,
And a means to escape,
All the current storms of evil,
Caused by sickness, death, and hate.

Yes, some see hope as fading,
Drowning in a flood of despair.
They see it as a sinking vessel,
A boat beyond repair.

But hope to me is like a feather,
Floating up to Heaven, so gracefully,
High above all those storm clouds,
And the raging of the sea.

Dedicated to Hope and her mother, Claire.

Psalm 71:10-14

The Flame

There is a flame,
In darkness of night.
There's a flame burning,
Flickering ever so bright.
It's igniting an eternal fire,
So deep within our souls,
An everlasting light,
For all to see.
Ever brighter it shines,
For every passing day it will find,
Another heart like yours and mine,
To set free.

Only the flame that comes from the Son, can bring us together and unite us as one, within the Father's fire above, of which all flames burn thereof.

Dedicated to my step brother, Brian.

Job 18: 5-6

The Lifeline

Drowning in a sea of emotion,
Grasping on to whatever I may find,
Amid the swirling darkening ocean,
Beneath the place where cumulonimbus clouds,
Are confined, and imprisoned within my mind.

I make an attempt to make sense of it all,
These feelings of loneliness and despair,
While many arms seem to grab and pull at me,
Leading me to God knows where.

As the thunder rolls between flashes of fire,
The wind pierces my head with its screams,
Accusations of satisfying ungodly desires,
And reminders of false hopes and broken dreams.

The rain as a flood,
Continues to pour down my face.
A whirlpool of fear and doubt envelop me.
As I am violently tossed by the raging sea,
I notice in a moment of time,
The strap tightening around me.

It's the lifeline, and it has been there all the while,
I had forgotten about it through the deceptions and trials.

All the storms that I have faced,
I have been pulled right on through.
After arriving at what seemed like my end,
This lifeline is bringing me back to you.

When you reach the end of your rope, feel the safety strap tighten around you, as Christ begins to pull you through life's greatest hardships and trials.

2 Timothy 3:11

Chad Joseph Thieman

The Water Bearer

Many have seen the sign in the stars,
Of a man who bears the water,
And many look for a new age to come,
But how many seek of His water?

If only they knew how to drink of it,
They could offer some to another,
And pour it forth into vessels more,
Until all become sister and brother.

First came the clay vessel, but now comes the water to fill it up, to overflowing. Indeed the Water Bearer will pour out his water upon all flesh. All vessels that can receive it, will receive it, and come into the knowledge of the truth. Many who were blind will now see!

Luke 22.10-11
John 4

We've Abandoned You

I can see your teardrops falling,
In the falling of the rain.
You can see the suffering here,
And you can feel our pain.

This ol' world keeps on turning,
And the sun, it keeps on burning,
But when will we start learning,
Lord, it's you we should be serving?

I can hear your mighty anger rage,
So high up in the thunderheads,
Because we've all abandoned you,
And have chosen ourselves instead.

This ol' world keeps on turning,
And the sun, it keeps on burning,
But when will we start learning,
Lord, it's you we should be serving?

After your anger begins to slow,
I can see your mercy in the rainbow,
For once again you calm the gusts,
And send your love out to forgive us.

This ol' world keeps on turning,
And the sun, it keeps on burning.
But when will we start learning,
Lord, it's you we should be serving?

Our God is not only a righteous judge but also a God of great love, patience, and mercy. Let us never forget that.

Mark 14:27

Chad Joseph Thieman

You Can Change the World

Some people say that one man can't change the world.
That is what the world wants you to think, but it's a lie.
People will come up with excuses to explain why,
They say the problems are too big, and don't even try.

Let me tell you about one man who did change the world.
Christ left Heaven, giving up more than we can imagine.
He came to this place, to serve in life and die in disgrace.
He did it for you and for me. He did it for all humanity.

Others will say that we don't need to change the world.
They think we should just sit back and let God change it.
Well, God is changing it right now,
And what great things people would accomplish,
If they would just open their eyes and ask Him how.

So let people see God in you, that they may turn to Him too.
Try hard to make a difference in every life,
And help put an ending to all the strife.
Make up your mind, work hard, and see all that you can do.
This world will be changed, and God is starting with you!

Dedicated to Jeanne and my other friends from PC3.

Even if you only change one person through Love, I tell you the truth, you have changed the entire world. For even if one pebble is thrown into a pond, the entire body feels the ripple effect that comes forth from it.

Philippians 2:13

The Love Collection

The hearts of men are waning cold,
Ignoring sage and prophet of old.
Such a lonely generation are we,
Living in the dark, unable to see.

I hear the dirges and children crying,
The trees are all rotting, wilting, dying.
I see the choice that lays before us,
Still there's a path that Love implores us.

Matthew 24:9-14

A Love Letter

This is a love letter from God's warrior to God's grace...

I've known love as tender as the morning,
Having felt it in a mother's embrace,
Having seen it in a child's smiling face,
Yet it never sent my heart soaring.

I've known love as hard as solid rock,
Immovable and stern in a father's word,
One that had to be quickly observed,
But it wasn't the reason this warrior fought.

Still there's a love, I have not yet known,
A love to me, that has yet to be shown.

As God's warrior, I have been through many trials,
Victoriously overcoming the Devil's wiles,
And coming full circle, I have changed many hearts,
But I still haven't found where truest love starts.

I wonder at times, *has God forgotten me?*
For at times the big picture is so hard to see.

Yet still I am here and keeping the faith,
Awaiting the day, when I finish the race,
Believing one day that my dreams will come true,
When at last I find their fulfillment in you.

I wrote "A Love Letter," from the perspective of one of God's warriors. It's about a believer who continues to fight the good fight and run the race of faith. He is always looking forward with great expectation and hope, to achieve his reward and crown of grace.

Psalm 42:9
Philippians 3:13-14

Chad Joseph Thieman

Give it Away

Love is the solution,
But you have to give it away.

Don't keep it for yourself,
It's time to share the wealth.
So look toward the coming new day,
And begin giving your love away.

For even if we gave it all,
Love would still remain,
Like a candle sharing its fire,
Its former glory, it retains.

Imagine how the world would be different,
If spreading love was our only aim.
In Heaven's eyes we would have lost nothing,
And yet many candles would gain a flame.

If you give your love away, you will change the world. Love is contagious, and when you set love in motion, it will change many hearts.

Dedicated to my brother, Craig, and the children of Moldova.

John 13:34

Love Has a Name

Love has a name,
Which few ever say.
A long time ago,
They threw it away.
Forgotten by most,
Until this very day.
God's sacred name,
Is Yah or Yahweh.
You see, God is love,
And through us He reigns.
Love is living Spirit,
And love will never change.
Christ, He was the first,
To come and proclaim,
Yah is Salvation.
It is Christ's holy name.
Through Yahshua's body,
Yahweh will reign.
For love is in Christ,
And love has a name.

Yahweh is the Hebrew name of God, and Yahshua is the Hebrew name for Jesus Christ. Yahshua actually means "Yah is Salvation". Yahshua is really pronounced Joshua in English, which still carries the meaning, "God is Salvation".

Dedicated to Rachel.

1 John 4:8

Love is All

Love is the Gospel,
And love is the law.
Love God and love neighbor,
Love fulfills it all.

Love is our only Savior,
And love is eternal life.
Love is our Father,
And love is in Christ.

Love is the Spirit,
That dwells in the light.
It created all things,
Love gives the breath of life.

Love is the only religion,
It is humble and meek.
Love requires sacrifice,
And reward it does not seek.

Love is true righteousness,
So love will never fail.
Love opens our eyes,
Love tears down the veil.

If God is really love,
Then what is an atheist?
But the one who believes,
That love doesn't exist.

It's true, we are not love,
But love we need most.
Love isn't prideful,
And love doesn't boast.

Love is living Spirit,
And love is our call.
Love must enter our temple,
Love will become all in all.

Dedicated to my step brother, Brandon

The foolishness of love is far better than the wisdom of worldly men.

1 John 4:21
1 Corinthians 15:28

Love is the Spirit

Love is the Spirit that we really need,
To break the chains of this anger and greed,
As we stand.

And love is the way, walking hand in hand,
While we enter into that promise land,
As we sing.

Love is the Sun arising within,
His love is moving us, like the wind,
As we dance.

And love is the Kingdom in those who believe,
The one who gives, is soon to receive,
As we dream.

Yeah, love is the answer to our every need,
Breaking the bonds of fear, hate, and greed.

Peace be upon the one who submits themselves to love entirely, for love is living Spirit and it gives birth to spirit in us. Invite the Spirit of love into the upper room of your heart.

Dedicated to my friend, Kristin.

2 Timothy 1:7

Love Requires Sacrifice

You might like someone a lot,
And want to keep them around.
You may tell them that you love them,
And like how it sounds.

But friend, if you don't give of yourself,
Then you have missed the whole thing.
You have to sacrifice for someone else,
To really know what love means.

What is love without some form of sacrifice? If you want to be a part of what God is doing, then start by investing your time, talents, and treasures into others.

Romans 12:1

Open Your Heart

Open your heart,
Let love flow in,
Seeping into the cracks,
Of one that is broken.

Living water absorbed,
In love, the heart is soaking.
A heart that was broken,
A heart now unbroken.

For out of the heart,
Living water is pouring.
Through the veins,
This water is coursing.

A life-giving fountain,
Gushing forth throughout,
From a heart that is open,
A heart now unbroken.

A renewed heart,
Love filling up within,
Overflowing for others,
So other hearts will mend.

More hearts filling up with love,
Soon all will be unbroken,
As these too, begin to overflow,
For those hearts, still left broken.

When we open our hearts to God and to others, we become fountains of His life giving water. This living water sustains the soul and spirit of a man, much in the same way that natural water nourishes the body.

John 7:38
2 Corinthians 6:11

What Love is Like

Love is like a well built vessel,
Sometimes, tossed wildly at sea.
Love is like a breath of fresh air,
Or a soft and gentle breeze.

Love is like a winding river,
As calm as it can be,
But don't let love catch you off guard,
For love still runs wild and free.

Love can open, most any door,
For love is often the key,
And although at times it may seem complicated,
Love is still simple as can be.

Love has a way of humbling us,
And bringing us down to our knees.
But love in the end, will help us stand,
Like the strongest of redwood trees.

When God brings you to your knees, know that He is doing so for your own benefit. Let your Heavenly Father strengthen you in your weakness that you may later stand strong and firm against the enemies of our God.

Dedicated to my step sister Allison, and her husband Lance.

Hosea 6:4

Chad Joseph Thieman

The Mother's Love Collection

Mother,

I hope you know that you are a blessing to me,
And throughout my life you always will be.
You are a special gift sent from Heaven above.
Oh, how very precious is a mother's love.

Thank you Mom, for always being there for me and covering me with your love, prayers, and blessings.

Proverbs 23:25

Every Day is Mother's Day

Mother's Day comes around only once a year,
Though it seems to me, mothers should be thought of,
Every single day throughout the year.

Every day they pray for their children,
And every day they shed a tear.
Every day they reflect on the memories, and help to shape new ones,
And every day they are burdened with fear.
Every day that they speak proudly of their children,
And every day the thought of their children, puts a sparkle in their eyes,
Is yet another day these mothers deserve,
To be blessed, honored, and recognized.

So though Mother's Day comes around only once a year,
And we may not always be near on this special day,
Let your heart find peace and comfort in,
How we love you in so many ways.

Being a mother is a full time job. When I say full time, I am not talking about a mere forty hour week. I am talking about a job that continues around the clock. Mother's Day is a travisty in one respect, because it gives mothers one day of honor, for an entire year of service. I wanted to write a poem that reminds people of what a mother's job entails. I hope that it will move people to take a little time every day, to remember and honor their mothers. So pause for a moment, and think about all that your mother has done for you, throughout your life.

Dedicated to my mother, with love.

Deuteronomy 5:16

Mothers are Angels in Disguise

Some take their mothers for granted,
They seem ordinary in their eyes.
But if they would look a little bit deeper,
They would be in for a real surprise.

You see a mother's love is our protection.
She hides us safely in her arms,
Guiding us in God's direction,
With discipline and firm correction.

Yet most cannot see this it seems,
They are looking with earthly eyes,
Blinded to all those spiritual things.

Therefore the gift of a mother is for the wise,
And those who can understand God's blessings.
For these look through with spiritual eyes,
To see God's angel beneath her disguise,
And understand the great love that she brings.

This is a poem that really needed to be written. Mothers are such a gift from God, yet most in today's generation have lost respect for their mothers. They have not seen or understood the gift of a mother. I hope that you can relate to this analogy above when thinking of your mother.

Dedicated to my loving mother.

1 Samuel 2:18-21

The Calling

I heard you calling in the night,
A voice across the great divide.

From your soul to my soul,
This message was sent.
In the middle of the night,
A great distance it went.

I promised to always be there for you,
And I felt that you needed me now.
I didn't mean to hurt you like that,
But my words, they did somehow.

You appeared in front of me,
As your face came to light.
Though my room was dark,
It soon became bright.

I held you close in my arms,
And we forgave each other,
A sorrow-filled son,
Holding his hurting mother.

Two spirits did meet,
For a moment in time.
I was there by your side,
The night your soul called out to mine.

Dedicated to my mother.

Ephesians 6:2-3

The Garden Poetry Collection

As I pass a small bass lake,
I stop and pause knowing whats at stake,
A chance to catch a timely glimpse,
A scene so rare and often missed,
Blossoming pink and white lotus flowers,
Upon that dark and murky, watery abyss.

Inspired by a small bass lake in Blowing Rock, NC.

Psalm 23:1-3

My Love is in Her Garden

My love is in her garden,
Blond hair streaming from her head.
She sits amidst flowering milkweed,
Beneath monarchs of gold and red.

Her gown is ever flowing,
A dress of Alice blue,
As she runs her fingers slowly,
Across the grass and morning dew.

Her beauty far surpasses,
All that I could ever dream.
Such tenderness and gentle love,
Are rarely ever seen.

She comes here quite often now,
To sit, reflect, and pray.
And whenever she starts to sing,
The doves come out to play.

The sun always turns its gaze,
To perceive this beauty below.
Its rays shine forth with softest light,
Upon her beautiful soul.

My love is in her garden,
And I have missed her mirth,
So I have come out to my love,
To sit and laugh with her.

Her secret garden is a wonderland of dreams,
where not everything is, as it may first appear or seem.

Song of Solomon 4:10-16
Isaiah 51:3

Chad Joseph Thieman

Rebecca Rose

In a garden of flowers,
At the center she grows,
A rose without thorns,
The reason,
Nobody knows.

It's captivating...I suppose,
That single red rose,
Standing out from the rest,
By the love that she shows.

Of all the flowers she's the best,
And faithfulness she will express.
For the day is coming soon,
When this rose will fully bloom.

Dedicated to my friend, Rebecca.

    A spiritual seed brings forth a spiritual rose.

Song of Solomon 2:2

The Garden of Light

I go to the garden of light,
In my tranquil dreams.
Moonbeams upon my eyes,
Are like sun drops in this scene.

Light and love flow over me,
Covering like the morning dew.
My spirit is filled with peace,
While I am created anew.

I see flowers roundabout me.
I can hear the bluebirds sing.
How I long to remain here,
In this tranquil dream.

Above me is a rainbow,
Though no storm has ever been.
Splendid are its colors,
Across the blue sky they bend.

I can feel the touch of God,
Just like the dancing leaves.
I sense His loving Spirit here,
In this cool and gentle breeze.

A little brook flows by me,
The spring of eternal life.
I hear a quiet whisper,
As the water reflects the light.

My heart is overjoyed,
My soul, it's so serene.
I wish I could stay forever,
In this tranquil dream.

Chad Joseph Thieman

I go to the garden of light,
In my tranquil dreams,
Where there is peace of mind,
And happiness it brings.

Dedicated to Grandma and Grandpa.

Genesis 2:9-11
Revelation 22:1-2

The Gardener

The other night I had a dream. I dreamt that I was walking through a beautiful garden with the Lord. As we walked along a cobblestone path, I noticed several kinds of flowers. There were vibrant roses, daisies, mustards, and lilies of every color. All of the flowers in the garden were in full bloom. I also noticed that there were weeds in the garden. The weeds grew at certain places in the garden and they were completely covered with thistles.

After seeing this, I realized that this garden belonged to me. I was to understand that all the flowers stood for the good deeds I had done in my life, and likewise, the weeds stood for all the evil things I had done. There was a flower for every time I had reached out to help a stranger in need, for each good word I had said, and for every Bible verse I had reflected on and read. But every time that I had judged, hurt, or lied to others, there grew a weed. I became afraid and started to tremble, for the weeds were choking the flowers and threatened to consume the entire garden.

Then the Lord spoke to me and said, "Do not fear my friend, if the weeds remained in your garden, it would die, but the Father knows this and sent me to tend to your garden. I am the Gardener, who pulls up all the weeds." The Lord continued, "I will pull them up and throw them out into the fire. The Father will not remember your weeds any longer. Soon your garden will be filled with flowers and that is how God will always see it. I will take away the weeds, but remember, you still need to plant flowers by your good deeds."

"The Gardener," was inspired by a similar dream I had. I really love this analogy of a garden, whereby the flowers represent good deeds and the weeds represent the bad. It really shows you the effects sin can have. Sin is likened to weeds that choke the flowers and destroy the garden. A healthy garden must be free of these destructive weeds.

Matthew 13:40
John 20:14-16

The Peony Parable

Oh, lovely peony flower,
How short is your bloom,
A mere couple weeks,
A few phases of moon.

You come and you go,
Few ever think twice,
Unknown to them,
Is the Kingdom of Christ.

Displaying three seeds,
Within your one flower,
You're a reminder to some,
Of love's mighty power.

Your first seed represents,
The planting of flesh.
Christ gained many others,
Through sacrifice and death.

Your second seed stands for,
His Spirit planted within,
As it grows and develops,
Within temples of men.

Your third seed symbolizes,
His living sacrifice,
Serving others each day,
Sowing into their lives.

Your seeds are three,
And Christ is like the peony.
He planted His body, Spirit, and life.
You represent the Kingdom of Christ.

No one can enter into the Kingdom of Heaven unless they come through Christ, for He is the Kingdom and the fullness thereof.

Dedicated to Dan, Jennings, and the rest of the guys in my small group.

John 14:5-6
1 Corinthians 15:37

The Suffering Love Collection

Love can be painful,
And love can burden the heart,
But all in all, love is worth the pitfalls,
If we continue to get up and play our part.

Proverbs 13:12

Happiness

I will wait for Happiness,
Though she may never show.
I will wait for Happiness,
Will she come? God only knows.

The years and miles are many,
That keep me from Happiness.
Though the memories of her are plenty,
To keep me holding on.

My heart, it stills feels empty,
When Happiness is gone.

*Dedicated to a special friend, whose name
means "Happiness."*

Job 7:7

Chad Joseph Thieman

Message in a Bottle

A message to my love I sent,
A poem with the sweetest words.
I told of the longing in my heart,
And the love imprisoned there from the start.

Then I rolled it up and stuffed it in,
A small glass bottle empty of gin.
I took the bottle, with my message in there,
Down to the riverbank where time lay bare.

I prayed this message, God would give her,
And threw it in that lonely river.
I thought, one day my love will find,
That bottle empty of gin,
And upon opening it up,
Discover my love there within.

The day I was turning in my final manuscript for this book, I saw a message posted on the wall at work. It was a message that came from a bottle. The Hilton hotel that I served banquets at, sits along the Cape Fear River. Some guy had written a message to his future wife, and had put the message in a bottle, and threw it into the Cape Fear. I would like to dedicate this poem to that guy. I hope that he finds the girl that he is longing for. Up until then, I did not have a dedication for this poem. The Lord still works in mysterious ways.

Dedicated to Josiah, I believe with all my heart that you will find her.

Romans 8:24-25

Words Left Unspoken

They say you should tell her,
The way that you feel.
They say you should let her know,
What is there in your heart.

So maybe I am only a fool,
With his heart that is broken.
I let you leave,
With words left unspoken.

I know it's probably too late,
To let you know now.
For now we are separated,
By so many miles.

But from my heart to your heart,
Consider it a token,
Of how I feel about you,
In these words left unspoken.

I have loved you from the beginning,
From the moment we first met.
I remember your smile,
And I could never forget.

When you left that one night,
From that dream I was awoken,
Because of those words,
The ones I left unspoken.

Sometimes the words that can hurt the most, are the ones left unspoken.

Dedicated to a special friend.

Psalm 34:18

Chad Joseph Thieman

Yesterday Again

Though the years have passed by, after many goodbyes,
I see you and then, it's like yesterday again.

Like we never did part, I've held you in my heart,
And I like it when... it feels like yesterday again.

Your eyes and your hair, that smile you had there,
I can never forget, the time we first met.

But like the water balloon that you threw,
The days have since flew.

And I have tried to forget, move on, but still yet,
I can't help but think of you.

Though the years have passed by, after many goodbyes,
I see you and then, it's like yesterday again.

Like we never did part, I've held you in my heart,
And I long for when... it feels like yesterday again.

*Now the road divides, you go one way and I'll go the other,
until one day our paths converge, and we truly find each other.*

Dedicated to a special friend.

Song of Solomon 2:14

The Grieving and Loss Collection

You left an imprint on our lives,
It's so hard for us to say good-bye,
But for awhile we must part.
We will always remember you,
You left your fingerprints on our hearts.

Dedicated to my great grandma and grandpa.

1 Thessalonians 4:13-18

A Shadow Befell Us

A shadow befell us one September morning,
When great terror set the cities to flame.
It was then that we all knew,
America would never again be the same.

On that fateful morning of nine-eleven,
There was heard a horrible crashing sound.
To those at the scene it felt like Armageddon,
The day the twin towers fell to the ground.

While the black smoke rose upward into the sky,
So did a multitude of terrible cries,
Ascending to Heaven, because for a moment,
We thought God had turned away His loving eyes.

A shadow befell us down at ground zero,
For there our nation mourned its greatest loss.
Many thousands died, including our heroes,
Who never once even counted the cost.

Some people searched through all the rubble,
In hopes that a few might have survived.
While some fell to their knees in prayer,
And others held their children and cried.

As I stood before the television I could see,
All the love coming out of that awful tragedy.
On that day, I saw people pray and unite,
And the shadow gave way, to God's holy light.

This poem is dedicated to those who died, and suffered loss from the collapse of the twin towers on 9-11, 2001.

Revelation 18:9-11

Cry Happy Tears

Some people are walking down life's lonely path,
Just going through the motions and breathing every breath.
It seems like they're barely able to live life at all,
Suffering each day for the love that they lost.

An innocent child, who was taken so young,
Or a loving grandmother, who once seemed so strong,
A sibling, a parent, a friend close to heart,
Where is the peace when our love ones depart?

They brightened our nights with their loving smiles,
And showered us with their kindness every day.
Though the years only lasted a short while,
Yet these memories we have, never will fade.

The purpose for their life has now been fulfilled,
And their legacy is left behind, for us to build.
They lived their life and obtained heavenly bliss,
Having left behind an eternal kiss.

A Spirit of love, so that we can understand,
That there are lasting implications here,
That we can't yet comprehend,
Like how the moving of love is fulfilling God's plan.

Friend, do not be like those who are without hope,
There is a promise of resurrection before the end,
And our loved ones will appear in the flesh once again.

So let your grieving for them be short my friend,
And keep the promise of scripture ever so near.
In Ecclesiastes you will find these comforting words,
"The day of one's death is better than the day of one's birth."

The death of the righteous are precious it's clear,
So let your mourning be short and cry happy tears.

*Dedicated to A.J. and Karson, in their loving memory
and to their mother, Margo and sister, Taylor.*

Psalm 116:15
Ecclesiastes 7:1-3

Healing Rain

Why you took her from me, I just don't know.
My family tells me I have to let go.
You know how much I have been trying,
But memories of my little girl, replay in my mind.

Heavenly Father let your Spirit here move,
And hear this prayer that I say unto you.
Please open your storehouse up in the sky,
And pour down upon me that rain from on high.
Hide these tears with the raindrops you send,
And let Heaven's rain help my broken heart mend.

I don't understand and it's so hard to see.
Father, I'm begging you please,
Hear my petition and send me a sign.
Let your rain fall on this hurting heart of mine.

Heavenly Father let your Spirit here move.
I close my eyes and lift my arms up to you.
Please open your storehouse up in the sky,
And pour down upon me that rain from on high.
Hide these tears with the raindrops you send,
And let Heaven's rain help my broken heart mend.

Dedicated to Jennifer, in her loving memory and to her mother, Cathy.

Acts 14:17

The Floating Rose

This poem is a tribute written for
a friend of mine, in honor of her mother.

As I stroll along the river today,
I carry this rose as a sign,
It represents my love for you,
And the legacy you left behind.

Your life is now lived through me.
Your image on earth still remains.
The rose represents the both of us.
You made Rose a part of my name.

As I cast this one into the river below,
I pray that you're watching and that you know,
I will love you forever and I promise to carry on,
Like this rose on the river that flows on and on.

Today is the day of your memorial,
I try to recall what you were like,
As the rose continues with the current,
And starts drifting out of sight.

I know one day I will see you again,
But until then I will glide with the wind,
Upon living water here,
In this river of life, love, and tears.

Dedicated to Judy. Her legacy lives on through her daughter, Rebecca.

Revelation 21:4

Chad Joseph Thieman

The Inspired Poet Collection

Long I sat in solitude,
Writing these simple poems of love,
While many around me sought success,
Without seeking it from above.

John 14:12

A Painter of Light

As an inspired poet, I help create a masterpiece,
Using living words filled with light.
Believing my work will never fade away,
I invest my time, my talent, and my life.

Like the painter, I have my canvas,
All those sad and lonely hearts.
This is where I paint the light,
And hope to leave my mark.

Simple poems are easily forgotten, I know,
If the readers aren't moved deep within.
So I paint these words with soft strokes and delicacy,
And let the Spirit of love guide my pen.

Though I may never have these poems displayed,
Framed nicely and hung in some museum,
I will continue to paint the light,
And with my brush spread love and freedom.

*My hope is to be a poet of light, and if these words come alive within
you, then you know that my legacy is true.*

Luke 8:16

Chad Joseph Thieman

The Divine Contest

Act 1

One day Satan appeared before the Lord,
Giving a challenge, he pushed for a quick retort.
"It will be me against man," he exclaimed,
"A poetry contest, to see who gets your name."

Indeed the Lord made His answer quick,
"Alright, Satan, you may have your wish,
Against any servant of mine you pick."

"Ha!," said the Devil, "I challenge this very night,
Young Joseph, a boy who can't even write."
Then Satan turned himself into an angel of light.

In an an instant He appeared to Joseph,
While at prayer, beside his bed,
Telling him of the challenge that be,
And all of the words in Heaven said.

In a vision, the Devil took him away,
And brought him into the wood,
Amidst crooked and rotting trees,
The only audience there,
Roundabout where they stood.

And Lucifer proclaimed, "Good luck my young lad,
I am the best poet that ever was had."
And he jumped up on an old, rotten stump and said,

Don't Tread Upon Me

Don't tread upon me, ye sons of man.
Scripture is merely the words of men.
From me to you, great knowledge came,
I have made you all creators,
And brought you the divine flame.

I am the Tree of Knowledge that will ever entice,
Evolution of consciousness awakens you to life.
There is no sin, only ignorance of your own will,
I let you taste, the flavors that pleasures fulfill.

Ye are all gods, who create your own world,
Listen not to this whimpering sage,
I will give you freely all the riches of the world,
In this new and coming Golden Age.

When he had finished, Lucifer jumped down from the stump,
And said to Joseph, "Now it's your turn chump."

Joseph said in reply, "Oh, Devil you will never learn,
God's name isn't something that one can earn,"
And Joseph stepped up to take his turn.

Act 2

The words Joseph spoke came from the Spirit,
And he lifted His voice, so all present could hear it.

The Tree of Life

Sons of men,

Seek ye only the Tree of Life,
That tree that bears good fruit.

This tree you seek is the body of Christ,
For only a watered tree will suffice.
If you believe that what I speak is true,
Then you shall share in this tree too.

For we are many branches you see,
With Christ being the trunk of this tree.

God's Spirit is the life giving water within,
Flowing up through David's roots.
The Spirit of love is filling this tree,
With a living fountain of youth.

When Joseph had finished he stepped down,
And the crooked trees began to straighten,
Because of the words of life heard there,
For these trees were lost men, now awakened.

That old Devil knew he had been beaten,
Giving a great shriek, he turned and fled,
As an angel appeared before Joseph,
Writing the Lord's name upon His head.

The trees of Eden were not ordinary trees by any means, they were symbolic. Lucifer's body is the Tree of Knowledge, which will be uprooted. Christ's body is the Tree of Life, a Spirit filled tree. Adam and Eve partook of the forbidden Tree of Knowledge instead of the Spirit filled Tree of Life. They were enlightened by the serpent, Lucifer, but they did not have the Holy Spirit of God within them; Therefore, they fell from their perfect state, and were kept from partaking of the Tree of Life. Christ suffered and died, so that we may partake of the Tree of Life, and have true oneness in the Father and Son. God shows us that we cannot save ourselves by knowledge and higher consciousness, but rather we have to come by faith in our Lord Jesus Christ, to receive the free gift of eternal life.

Ezekiel 31:1-18, Revelation 2:7, Revelation 22:1-4

The Poet in Me

Some have called me a poet,
Though I would have to disagree.

It may have been my hand that wrote it,
But the Spirit of love was guiding me.

Though the reader may never know it,
I tell you this with all honesty.

Many poems have failed before it,
When nothing was there to inspire me.

The real Author is the truest of poets,
And by His words, He always will show it.

I am only God's instrument you see,
Yahweh my Father is the poet in me.

Many people have told me that "The Poet in Me," though it is a simple poem, has a deep and profound meaning to it. I believe that God does inspire, and that His words are very much alive.

1 Thessalonians 2:13

Chad Joseph Thieman

The Poet's Pen

How mighty is the poet's pen,
No enemy of his will continue to stand.

The true poet's words will always suffice,
Without the spilling of blood or loss of life.

Through his prose his influence lasts,
And when his enemies long have passed,
The poet's words will yet hold fast.

For the true poet is inspired from above,
And brings to the reader living words of love.

Sharper are these than any two-edged sword,
Subverting regime, emperor and warlord.

Even soul and spirit these words do part,
Like a sharpened arrow straight through the heart,

No better option has one to fight,
For the hearts of men, a poet's words ignite.

And all that was thought concealed,
In latter days again revealed.

In this way a poet's words prevail,
Tearing down the darkest veil,
To bring life and healing from God's living well.

Dedicated to my friend, Robert (Humanitarian Poet).

Psalm 45:1-5

The Charity Collection

Give shelter to a homeless man.
Give a home to the little orphan.
Give comfort to the lonely widow.
Give a coin to the man with the fiddle.

Those who do not give freely while they are yet poor, will be no more generous, if they were to become rich.

Luke 3:11

Charity

Some see charity as a way to benefit self,
It makes them feel good and look good as well.
They only give with the return in mind,
And see their action as oneness defined.

They look for the reward that they might receive,
But if that is their attitude, then they are deceived.
For charity is not giving to elevate one's self,
Nor is it defined as spreading the wealth.

The true meaning of charity is sacrifice you see,
Lifting up others, not thinking of me.
Christ led by example with real humility,
A much needed attitude found in true charity.

Some people who claim enlightenment, love others without sacrifice. This is a phony love, a love that does good because it will benefit self. Those who truly know God, know that love and sacrifice go hand in hand. These invest in others for the sake of helping others and not for the reward that they will receive later. You must have a humble heart, with good and honest intent. Follow the Lord's example. Love is not selfish, but selfless. By your love you will be known. Self sacrifice in your daily lives, will bring glory to God.

Hebrews 13:16

Give it Away

Love is the solution,
But you have to give it away.

Don't keep it for yourself,
It's time to share the wealth.
So look toward the coming new day,
And begin giving your love away.

For even if we gave it all,
Love would yet remain,
Like a candle sharing its fire,
Its former glory, it retains.

Imagine how the world would be different,
If spreading love was our only aim.
In Heaven's eyes we would have lost nothing,
And yet many candles would gain a flame.

Love alone makes one great, so love wholeheartedly.

John 13:34

Giving in Secret

Do your giving in secret,
Changing hearts one by one.
Don't wear your accomplishments,
Or proclaim what you've done.

Don't seek out acknowledgment,
Never accept payment or reward.
Just keep it between yourself,
Your Heavenly Father and your Lord.

Consider giving like sowing a small seed,
You won't see the effect for a good little while.
Be patient my friend and keep planting your seed,
When the critics come just look at them and smile.

Remember, your Heavenly Father will repay you,
For all the good in life that you've done.
Until then just be patient my friend,
You will know when your harvest has come.

I know that many of you sow in the physical realm giving to charities and helping the poor, but how many of you sow in the realm of the Spirit? If you plant a physical seed you will reap a physical harvest, but if you plant the Spirit, you will reap the Kingdom of Heaven!

Dedicated to my friend, Renae

Matthew 6:4

Chad Joseph Thieman

The Bible Collection

The Lord told me to go to Nineveh,
But I did not do as He wished.
I sailed my boat in the opposite direction,
And got swallowed by a fish. - Jonah

Jonah 1:1-17

His Footprints

The Messiah walked on water,
But Peter sunk with haste.
Come to Christ, he could not,
For he lacked greatly in faith.

The wind it blew so strong,
And the waves, they were so vile,
Yet Christ told him to come,
With the faith of a little child.

But Peter became terrified,
And sinking, he threw out his hand.
Christ shook His head and had mercy,
And reached down to rescue the man.

Sometime later Christ walked beside him,
As they walked down a stretch of beach.
He encouraged and gave him instruction,
"Peter, please feed my sheep."

And to make sure this time,
His disciple could follow God's plan.
The Messiah left His footprints,
Behind, in the sand.

Let us follow in the footsteps of the Lord, letting His footprints guide us, always.

Dedicated to my friend, Preston.

Matthew 14:22-33

Chad Joseph Thieman

In the Whispers

I was in a cave, upon the Mount,
When a mighty whirlwind came about.
I asked the Lord if it be He,
But answered not, the Lord did He.

So I prayed and kept awake,
Until there came a great earthquake.
I asked the Lord if it be He,
But answered not, the Lord did He.

So I started to pray once again,
And down came a pillar of fire, from Heaven.
I asked the Lord if it be He,
But answered not, the Lord did He.

My patience there was wearing thin,
When by my way, came whispers of gentle wind.
I covered my face and went on forth,
For in the whispers, came my Lord.

Prayer is simply talking to God and listening for that one still voice. There have been many times throughout my life that I have gone out into nature, to walk and talk with God. It is important that we find time to quiet our souls, so that we can really listen and hear His Spirit speaking.

Dedicated to Uncle Chris and Aunt Carol.

1 Kings 19:11-13

Sometimes I Think About That Cross

Sometimes I think about that cross,
Standing up on Calvary's mound.
I see the women crying there,
And roman soldiers all around.

On the cross I see my Savior,
So weak and so very torn.
His hands are pierced with nails,
And His crown is covered with thorns.

His blood is like a scarlet robe,
Running from His head down to His feet,
And the only ones who seem to care,
Are the women below Him who weep.

I pretend to be the centurion,
Standing there below the cross,
Looking up into His eyes,
When Jesus died and paid the cost.

When I am burdened in my life,
I just think about that cross.
I ponder what the Lord did there,
What we gained and what He lost.

Let us never forget that the Father gave His Son to suffer and die for us. Our Lord showed us that love requires sacrifice. His offering was a flesh and blood offering, an atonement for sin that would bring us to "at-one-ment" in Him. Therefore my brethren, do not put your trust in yourselves, as though you could save yourselves, but rather put your trust in God. Look up, for your redemption is nigh.

Dedicated to my friends at Mount Calvary, in Wilmington, NC.

John 6:40
John 19:16-30

Chad Joseph Thieman

The Kingdom of Heaven

In parables Christ spoke of the sower and seed,
So that some could hear and yet not receive.

The message hidden within was for only His sheep,
Those who are humble and those who are meek.

He showed us the Kingdom is right here on earth.
Christ's body was a mustard seed planted in the earth.

Of those in the Kingdom, Christ was the first.
He sacrificed His body, that a multitude be birthed.

The Kingdom of Heaven will grow into a large tree,
Watered by God's own Spirit, filling all who believe.

It was planted by Christ, His body was the good seed,
But an enemy came in and he sowed some weeds.

Satan planted his body upon the earth just the same.
When the Angels saw this, to their Master they came.

The Master said pulling up tares could harm the wheat,
And told them to wait until the harvest was complete.

Then the weeds would be gathered together and burned,
When Christ comes into His Kingdom at His return.

The Son of Man will then reap all that He has sown,
And gather together His sheep from both of His folds.

At the fullness of His Kingdom all will understand,
That God's Spirit is to dwell within the temple of man.

Now a shaft of wheat cannot become a tare and likewise a tare cannot become wheat. Each is of its own kind and has come from its own seed. So know the seed by what it produces. It is well known by wheat farmers that tares must remain with the wheat until the harvest. The reason for this, is that the tares and wheat look exactly alike, and you cannot tell the difference by looking at them. After they have matured and are fully grown, the poisonous tares will become physically different in appearance, and the harvesters will be able to recognize them, for what they really are.

Matthew 13:24-30
Matthew 15:13

The Mark of the Beast

Please do not think me crazy, as people sometimes do,
For I am sometimes criticized, for speaking what is true.

Just read the Scriptures and consider, wise those words within,
And listen to the living Spirit, coming forth from Godly men.

Before too long the truth will come, and you will understand,
The Devil's system has always been, the monetary system of man.

If you doubt this, look on the back of a one dollar bill,
There you'll find Lucifer's all seeing eye, hovering above the pyramid still.

The British Royals in Wales have control of the world's banking cartels,
Their flag pictures a Great Red Dragon, a warning Revelations did tell.

There is a time now coming soon, when you will have to choose my friend,
Whether or not to receive a mark upon your forehead or in your hand.

So prepare yourself to make this choice, to deny all the riches of man,
For you see, universal wealth, is Lucifer's ultimate plan.

Soon the political and business world will look like a kingdom of light,
Like an angel that has come down from Heaven or the sun at its height.

Do not be deceived my brethren, for this is a grand delusion,
Many will depart from the faith because of these coming illusions.

Do not receive a mark in your forehead that covers your spiritual eye,
Or a stamp in the palm of the hand, for it is all one big lie.

Do not accept a UPC, a microchip, or any symbol of electronic control,
By taking it you'll become rich on Earth but in the end, forfeit your soul.

What good is it to gain it all and have everything this world has to offer,
If you become a slave to the system and a cold hearted, evil scoffer?

Now if you refuse the mark, they may say you reject God and must die,
But die with joy and thanksgiving my friend, for it is you who are all the wise.

For soon the greedy with all their riches, will perish off the Earth,
And love will awaken, those who found in God, true and lasting worth.

There will be no more need of money, when the Kingdom of Christ comes into its fullness. After the Spirit of love enters into all men, then all will give freely to one another, and no one will go without. Remember, Christ said that His Kingdom is not of this world. It is not a monetary system at all. It is the sowing and reaping system of the Spirit.

Revelation 12:9-11
Revelation 13:1-18

The New Jerusalem

(Inspired by St. John's Revelation)

From up on a mountain high,
I saw God's city come down from the sky.
Oh, how the new Jerusalem shone,
Just like the precious jasper stone.

The city had a great wall,
With three pearl gates on each side.
At every gate, there stood an angel,
One for each of Israel's twelve tribes.

The city walls had twelve foundations,
On each was an apostle's name.
Its light shone forth on all saved nations,
And kings brought glory when they came.

The crystal clear city was made of pure gold,
And so was the city's transparent road.
The only temple there, was the Great I Am,
And all the light came from the Lamb.

On either side of the river was a tree,
One in the middle of the road made three.
There the Tree of Life had sprung its roots,
And every season it gave of its fruits.

Then I saw a pure river of water run,
Living water from God and His Son.
From God's glorious throne it flowed,
Down throughout that city of gold.

All that God showed me is true,
Heaven and earth will be made new.
The city is for those in the Book of Life.
The new Jerusalem will be the Lamb's wife.

Envision it in your mind, the new Jerusalem coming down from Heaven!

Dedicated to my friend, Pascal.

Revelation 21:10-27

The Two Olive Trees

Here stand two Olive trees,

Those two sons of fresh oil.

In their midst a great lamp stand,

Which partakes without spoil,

Keeping its flame by the overrunning oil,

From these two trees, ever so loyal.

Two witnesses of the Spirit that be,

Opening the eyes of a church that can't see,

And of these upright Olive trees,

Which are numbered here at two.

One may like to entertain the thought,

Of being one of the prominent two.

The two olive trees of the Lord, come to bring a great harvest in the last days. Their testimony is like one of fire. Those who love God will be tested by this fire, and they will be made as pure gold; while those people who attempt to harm these two witnesses, will be destroyed by the fire that comes forth, from their mouths.

Zechariah 4:11-12

Until There Was You

Until there was you, I traveled my own road,
Wearing down others who carried my load,
Not concerned with the strings that I pulled,
Or the way my actions would later unfold.

I didn't think twice when fulfilling my desires,
I didn't think, I would get burned by that fire.
Until there was you, myself alone I admired.
In the darkness I walked, weary and tired.

Until there was you, I never found rest,
I buried my talents, locked in a chest,
And spent my money, until none was left.
Until there was you, I was in quite a mess.

Until there was you, to and fro I did roam,
And when I fell, I was dashed by the stone.
Until there was you, I lived on my own,
But when I found you, you welcomed me home.

You embraced and held me, calling me son,
Though I was lost, that prodigal one.

If you have been living life as a prodigal son, I would like to invite you to come home to the Father and dedicate your life to Christ. Let the scriptures be your guideposts, leading you along the pathway of life.

Dedicated to my friend, Stanley.

Luke 15:11-24

The True Religion Collection

Religion is not oneness except within Christ,
For those of His body, who believe in sacrifice.
It is these who discover, true religion is love,
Seeking out the Father, being born from above.

My religion is a four letter word. - Love

Ephesians 4:4
John 17:20-23

A Church Without Walls

I would like to take a moment to share with you an experience I had, one Friday night this past June. I went downtown to pass out some of my poetry, while a friend played worship songs on his guitar and sang. We were on the corner of Front and Market Street, in downtown Wilmington. It felt a little strange at times being out there witnessing like that, but we kept it up, believing in these talents that God had blessed us with.

As people passed by, I handed out a small packet of my poetry and asked, "Can I bless you with some poetry today?" Though some seemed annoyed by this kind gesture, many accepted my little packet of poetry with gratitude. Some people even came back later to thank me and my friend, for everything we were doing. An hour passed and then two. Soon we were joined by two more friends of ours. We all started singing "I Can Only Imagine" and "Nothing But The Blood of Jesus," though not too loud at first. It seemed for a moment that the Kingdom of Heaven was opening up before our eyes. We felt like little children singing on the street corner. A bird flew down and began flying all around us, and people were noticing the glow on our faces. You could just feel a reality shift.

Before too long, a couple more people decided to join in and we got a little bit louder. Then two guys on guitar asked to join us. Soon a church worship leader noticed what we were doing and approached us, asking if he could play on one of the guitars. Before we knew it, we had nine people, three of them on guitar. We were worshiping God and people on all four corners of the main crossroad could easily hear us. Young teenagers were walking by singing along. People were rolling down their car windows to hear the music and to sing praises to God. It was one of the most amazing experiences that we had ever experienced. Our church was on a street corner. Our church was one without walls. We were having a worship service in the center of downtown on a Friday night, and lives were being impacted and God was being glorified. We had brought a light to the city for a moment in time. We stepped out into the darkness to shine the light of Christ and all of this at a time when the bars began to draw crowds. It was spiritual warfare on the highest level and hearts were being changed.

I never could of imagined that could all come about because two people stepped out in faith and did something that no one else would do. God used us, and He drew people to us. I know without a doubt that we made a difference that night. I know people who never stepped foot in a church before, saw for the first time, the joy, love, happiness, and unity, that we have in Christ Jesus.

Dedicated to my friends, Kevin, Ward, and Hillary. I am very thankful that I got to share in this moment with you.

I belong to a church without walls. My church is the body of Christ. The people in this church come into agreement; they are of one flesh, one mind, and all partake of the same Spirit. Denominations are too often used as a means of segregation. Those who attempt to segregate and divide the body are working against us and the oneness that we have found in Christ. The true church is the family of Christ, these are spirit filled believers. The walls that men have put up and maintained, will come crumbling down. A church without walls that is what we are. Only after we leave the temples of man behind, will the true harvest come.

Matthew 10:27, Matthew 18:20, 1 Corinthians 10:17, Ephesians 4:4-6

Bear the Cross

I challenge you to bear the cross,
Each and every day,
Standing as a witness of truth,
Living out all that you believe and say.

For some the cross around their neck,
Is the only one that they can bear.
So please keep your faith in check,
If a cross you choose to wear.

Don't think a symbol will prove your faith,
Or that wearing one will bring you grace.
For the Father works through love and spirit,
And to receive truth, one must see and hear it.

So live like Christ in your everyday life,
Instead of wearing religion on your sleeve.
A necklace, bracelet, t-shirt, or tie,
These are earthly, man made things.

And before you make the cross of light,
An idol for display,
Try living by the Spirit's might,
And be the light that points the way.

Many people wear a cross but so very few are willing to bear their cross. Bearing the cross, is putting the desires of the flesh to death daily and then taking on the burdens of others. Martyrs plant their flesh for the sake of the Kingdom of God, but we can do so daily by surrendering our lives, to bring glory to our Father in Heaven.

Luke 14:27

Chad Joseph Thieman

God Just Turns Everything Upside Down

(This poem is not as it first appears, you must read through to the end)

Jesus Christ is the way
All believers will say
You were bought for a price
God's Son gave up His life
Jesus Christ suffered and died on the cross
These things are all lies and completely false
I make my own reality and rules
God is only for fools
I can choose what is wrong and right
I am the God of my own life
It is laughable to believe such things like
God created you and me
Only Jesus Christ can set us free
Those born of love will never die
We must repent of lust and pride
Whether you like it or not, the real truth is this
We are the result of evolution and God doesn't exist
Death is the end of your life
Darkness has victory over light
God is only a fairytale and a crutch for the weak
It is foolishness to turn the other cheek
Only the ignorant will say
I will carry my cross every day
Jesus Christ is the only way
God is changing my heart
The reality is
My life is broken

This is the mindset of the worldly person, until they experience God. Then He turns their world completely upside down, reversing all of what they once believed. On the next page is the same exact poem but completely reversed. This is what you would read, if you read the above poem starting at the bottom, reading each line going up.

My life is broken
The reality is
God is changing my heart
Jesus Christ is the only way
I will carry my cross every day
Only the ignorant will say
It is foolishness to turn the other cheek
God is only a fairytale and a crutch for the weak
Darkness has victory over light
Death is the end of your life
We are the result of evolution and God doesn't exist
Whether you like it or not, the real truth is this
We must repent of lust and pride
Those born of love will never die
Only Jesus Christ can set us free
God created you and me
It is laughable to believe such things like
I am the God of my own life
I can choose what is wrong and right
God is only for fools
I make my own reality and rules
These things are all lies and completely false
Jesus Christ suffered and died on the cross
God's Son gave up His life
You were bought for a price
All believers will say
Jesus Christ is the way

Isn't it amazing how God can turn our ideas upside down and make even the most prideful among us, as humble as a little child?

John 14:6

God's Keys to Success

My friend, God's keys to success are not complex,
And never were they, secrets to be kept.

Our faith must exceed our doubts and our fears,
Faith comes by hearing, so open your ears.

We must give up negativity, anger, and strife,
Repent of our sin, and surrender our life.

So ask for the Father's Spirit, to fill you within,
And live by His Spirit, rejecting all sin.

Then through your actions, His love will manifest,
As you put to death, the desires of the flesh.

Though life is not always easily understood,
You can find joy in the pain, it works for your good.

No matter how bad things may sometimes appear,
Always remain positive, and cast away fear.

Seek Godly wisdom, and put others first,
By investing in others, you're breaking the curse.

Always love your enemies, for they need it most,
Humble yourself, for love doesn't boast.

Don't be ashamed of God at all,
Promote your Heavenly Father, first and most of all.

Put your talents to work, and give Him the glory,
And He will use others, to help write your Kingdom story.

Before reaping a harvest, there are seeds you must sow.
Always see your glass, as being completely full.

Surround yourself with those who believe,
Ask Your Heavenly Father for whatever you need.

But do so in the right Spirit, not in selfishness or greed,
Then to the Father, much glory you'll bring.

Always seek out positive and believing friends,
Ask others for help, who have God's Spirit within.

Say it out loud, all that you would like to receive,
And remain determined, to accomplish your dreams.

Take every good opportunity that comes around,
With every step of faith, you're gaining some ground.

Believe God will give you, whatever you ask for,
Envision it daily, and keep knocking on that door.

Surround yourself with reminders of your goal every day,
Remain near to God's Spirit, and He will show you the way.

Live out each day, as though you have already been blessed,
While you wait for the day, when God sends your harvest.

Isn't it strange, how sometimes you cannot fulfill your own needs, but you can always help to fulfill the needs of others? The reason for this is because you are to be the answer to their success, and they are to be the answer to yours. Indeed many never find success because they seek success in and through the world's system, instead of seeking it through the Kingdom of Heaven. The world cannot keep success from those in Christ, who work together and believe that they have already achieved it.

2 Chronicles 26:5, Psalm 1:2-4, John 14:13-14

God's Temple

God's temple isn't made from brick or stone,
Its origin is somewhat unknown.

It wasn't fashioned by human hands,
Nor was it built by the devices of man.

It was never drawn up on blueprint plans,
And its foundation isn't built into land.

There is no cross or high-reaching steeple,
Because it consists of a body of people.

God's temple isn't made from brick or stone,
He made His temple of flesh and bone.

The temple is Christ and the body of man,
And the Spirit enters in fulfilling God's plan.

One temple wears a cross upon it and the other bears the cross upon it. Brothers and sisters, do you not know that the true temple is Christ, and that He laid down His temple and took it up again? He did this so that you could also become temples of God and a part of His body. Our bones are to be the stones of God's temple and our flesh, the tent of His Spirit.

John 2:19-22
1 Corinthians 3:16

The Jesus Glasses

I came across a crippled, old man, as I strolled the park one day. He was sitting in his wheelchair feeding the pigeons. As I approached him, he greeted me with a smile, and I could see he had a strange glow about him. I asked him how he found his joy, peace, and contentment in life. The old man just laughed and handed me his sunglasses. He told me to try them on and see. I thought that he was just another foolish, old man, a crazy dreamer bound to his chair. I told him I didn't have time for his silly games and walked on by.

It was weeks later before I could find time to walk that park once again. You see, my schedule was filled with business meetings, Wall Street dealings, and taking care of my personal possessions. I really had little time left. After all, I was a successful business man and success comes with its sacrifices. This time it was starting to get dark, so I kept up my pace. It wasn't long before I noticed that crippled, old man, sitting under a lamp-post. He was still wearing those same sunglasses. I knew the man could not possibly be able to see through those glasses, after all the sun had already set.

I stopped and asked him, "Sir, I don't mean you any disrespect, but how can you possibly see anything with those sunglasses of yours?" The man smiled at me and said, "These glasses are magical glasses."

I couldn't keep a straight face, I burst out into laughter, and asked, "Have you lost your mind old man, magical glasses?"

"I understand why you think me crazy, only those who believe can see through these glasses," answered the old man.

"Believe in what?" I asked sarcastically.

"Why, believe in Jesus of course, these are Jesus glasses," replied the old man. "Those in the dark, see those of the light as fools because they are still in the dark and cannot yet see the light. When a person sees the light, their eyes will be opened. The light of all men is Christ, the sower and the seed of the Kingdom of Heaven on Earth."

Finally, I had heard enough. I grabbed the sunglasses from him and looked through them myself, but I couldn't see a thing. It was dark as midnight looking through those glasses. I took them back off and said, "man you are crazy," and tried to hand them back, but he refused to take them back and told me to hang on to them. I took the glasses with me, went back to my convertible and drove home.

Early the next morning I was on my way to work, wearing the sunglasses. The first thing I witnessed was a car accident about thirty yards ahead of me. A suburban hit a small S-10 pick-up truck, and blocked the road for over twenty minutes. When I finally got to work, I pulled in front of my office building and was approached by two dirty bums trying to get money out of me. I advised the men to try working for a living and brushed them off. I was already fifteen minutes late and I didn't have any time for this. I took off the sunglasses as I went inside. Being superstitious, I figured that they were somehow bringing me bad luck. As a matter of fact, every time I had them on, bad things seemed to happen all around me.

About a month later I ran into that crippled, old man in the park again, and I questioned him about the glasses. "Sir, didn't you say that these glasses brought you joy and contentment? All I have witnessed are bad circumstances and problems, every single time I put them on."

The old man replied, "My friend, it is not what you see with those glasses that count but what you do with what you see that really matters. You see, Jesus taught us to help other people and plant seeds into their lives. The Kingdom of Heaven is all around you, but to enter into it you must first become like a little child and believe. Jesus showed us that planting seeds of love would trigger a chain of events that would change many lives, including your own. Next time you witness these things, just do what Jesus would do and you will see your life begin to transform."

This time something in this man's message took hold of my heart. I promised him that I would try to change my attitude and give the glasses another chance.

The next day, I put the sunglasses on once again and headed to work. On the way there, I spotted a man pushing his stalled car off the road. His wife was in the driver's seat, turning the wheel. I pulled off to the side of the road and helped the couple get their car out of the street. After we got the car moved, I hurried on to work, for I was already five minutes behind. This time, though, I decided to keep the glasses on throughout the day, which brought some really strange looks my way. Every time someone asked me why I was wearing sunglasses, I told them, "These are my Jesus glasses!" I tried to explain it but many just thought it was some kind of gag. They all knew I was a bit crazy anyhow.

I wasn't at the office long, before opportunity started knocking. My secretary received a phone call that her mother was being evicted from her apartment. She was in tears, so I asked her where her mother lived. At lunch time I went to the apartment office and paid the rent, without my secretary knowing what I had done. Then, I pulled up to my favorite diner on the corner of 5th and Main. I sat down in my usual booth. Through the glasses I saw a pregnant woman approach to take my order. After a good meal and a somewhat lengthy conversation, I realized that the child would be number three for this single mother. So when she wasn't looking, I dropped a hundred on the table and left.

I continued throughout the day, giving encouragement to those who needed it the most, thanking my employees for all their hard work, and explaining the Jesus glasses to others. I even stuck a twenty in the return coin slot of a Coke machine, to make someone's day. I felt like I was a different person and I was.

Over the course of the next few weeks, I laid out a plan to invest some of my belongings into the lives of others, who were in need of them. I realized that my possessions had weighed me down and they had greater worth if I invested them in others, or sold them to help the poor. I continued planting into the Kingdom around me and investing what needed to be invested.

One day I even stopped by to see that nice, elderly gentleman in the park. I handed him a brand new pair of designer sunglasses. I explained to him how he helped me and the lives of countless others. Before leaving the park, I came across a small child with some colored chalk. I helped her write the message, "God Loves You," across the sidewalk, for all the lonely passers-by.

Now, twelve years later, I am living in a whole new world. Every time I am in need, the need seems to be met. Some stranger will appear with a pair of sunglasses to lend me a hand or bless me with a gift. I have to laugh at those who don't believe because I have everything that I will ever need, not to mention a lot more free time to enjoy the magnificent view, through my Jesus glasses.

Chad Joseph Thieman

Every day there are people who are placed in your path and it is no coincidence that they are there. If you want to participate in the Kingdom of Heaven, then ask for God's Spirit, look for these people, and invest in them. Each time that you invest in one of these with love, you will change the world. Love will trigger a domino effect, each action will create a reaction, and love will continue to spread. If only people understood the impact that they can have on others and the world, each and every single day. Every day there are thousands of opportunities but sadly most of these are passed by. When will people start to see that by investing in others, we can change many lives?

Matthew 13:1-23
Matthew 19:13-28

The Desire and Passion Collection

Every day I will put them to death,
Hang on the cross all that is left,
Of my passions and desires,
And the lusts of my flesh.

Don't seek to fulfill the desires of the flesh. Seek and fulfill the desires of the Spirit. The flesh and its works will perish off the earth, but the works of the Spirit will bring lasting reward.

Luke 9:23-26
1 Corinthians 15:31

Driven

Driven away by physical desire,
You know what you want,
And seek to acquire.

Chasing your dreams,
But for selfish reasons.
No, you don't understand,
Your troublesome seasons.

Living for yourself,
Is like walking a live wire,
Chasing all that you want,
While burning with fire.

Seeking fame and success,
And material greed,
Pursuing what you want,
And not what you need.

What you see is a mirage,
While running to pleasure.
Chasing an image,
You give up what matters.

Try asking for God's Spirit,
And be driven by love.
All that you need,
Is contentment from above.

You have to tear down an old bridge before you can build a newer, stronger, and more glorious one; but tenderness, firmness, and love are necessary at all times.

Acts 14:15

Chad Joseph Thieman

Overcoming Lust

To overcome lust you must first understand,
It is the worship of flesh and the worship of man.
It is ignoring God's Spirit and His holy truth,
For self-seeking pleasure that benefits you.

We are to yearn for the Spirit and not for the flesh,
And to remain pure, apart from the rest.
Though we may stumble from time to time,
We must never let lust take control of our minds.

Only in marriage between a woman and a man,
Will lust play a role in God's unique plan.
Lust outside of marriage is always a sin,
At sometime or another we've all given in.

If we ask for God's Spirit, He promises rest,
For His Spirit alone leads to true righteousness.
Only if we have the Spirit of love living within,
Can we overcome lust and the temptation to sin.

The greatest weapons used to overcome temptation is having love for God, others, and yourself; also having the fear of God, to obey His commandments; cutting out of your life, all things that may cause you to be tempted; and being well versed in the scriptures, so that you can recall them in times of struggle. These are the only means by which one can truly escape and overcome temptation. Remember, the flesh is weak, but the Spirit is willing.

Romans 13:14

Passion's Fire

All are born of flesh,
But not all are born of love.
Those whom Heaven birthed,
Are children from above.

All others spend their lives,
Chasing physical desires,
Persistently throwing fuel,
Upon that lustful fire.

Feeding their passions more every day,
As the flame burns higher and higher.
Forgetting true love's way,
And all that it requires.

They do not seek the Spirit of love,
Pleasure is all they care to acquire,
Like hands that grab hold and cannot let go,
Due to a dangerous current's electric flow.

Their situation looks ever dire,
Stuck to this deadly, live wire.
There is nowhere else for them to go,
These obtain the world but forfeit their soul.

If you lost your innocence somewhere in the past, then stop, turn around, and search diligently for it that you may find it once again.

1 Corinthians 6:15-20

Chad Joseph Thieman

The Broken Compass

Cursed is this compass, at sea I did find,
Better off had it been, if I were born blind.
For this compass of desire leads me nowhere,
Pointing its needle, in every direction I care.
Spinning wildly, with unstable magnet within,
Clockwise, counterclockwise, and clockwise again.
Around and 'round, three-hundred sixty degrees,
Leaving me with thirty-two points of possibility.
If only I could get these bearings here straight,
I wouldn't be left with such questionable fate.

    Don't be like a broken compass, spinning wildly. Find direction in Christ, and walk in His ways.

Romans 8:5-11

The Wedding and Marriage Collection

Await my arrival, my virgin, my bride,
Your bridegroom is coming and will remain by your side.

2 Corinthians 1:3

A Mystical Honeymoon

We walk the shore of a foreign land,
With tender strides across the sand,
Holding each other close with gentle hands,
You are my princess, and I am your man.

Like a slow dance in the moonlit night,
Our bodies sway beneath soft, cascading light.
Like dancing stars, in our own right,
The Heavens look down, beholding the sight.

I pull you closer, and move the hair from your face,
And lay you down gently, with tender embrace.
One hand glides slowly, untying your lace,
As we begin making love, in this mystical place.

I hope this poem will take the reader to that mystical place, where love abides.

Song of Solomon 8:3

The Marriage

The biblical structure of marriage,
Represents the church and Christ.
With Christ the loving husband,
And the church, His humble wife.

We respect His lead and authority,
And for Christ we always yearn.
He loves us and sacrificed for us,
And listens to all our concerns.

Yet marriage isn't just a bond of two,
It is more like a union of three.
The Father's Spirit must dwell inside,
Of this newly joined body.

If your marriage doesn't follow,
What scripture says is true,
And you reject this biblical model,
To make your marriage about you,

Then you won't find fulfillment my friend,
For you lack humility.
Without God's guiding Spirit,
A successful marriage, you'll never see.

Marriage is a bond that must be strengthened daily. Every day there will be trials or troubles, but the key to getting through them, is by coming together in Christ and letting God's Spirit move within.

Dedicated to Daniel and Amy.

You guys had one of the most beautiful weddings that I have ever seen, and I have seen many of them. I pray that you will remain faithful to God and to each other, living as a true representation of Christ and His church.

Ephesians 5:23
Romans 1:25-27

The Wedding Poem

I wish the best for the both of you,
May all your hopes and dreams come true.
Many good times will come, you can be sure.
Those are the memories that you must capture.

When you are troubled, look to the sky,
And remember God will help you to fly.
Always hold each other tight,
And pray together day and night.

Then your life will be a great success,
And your future will bring happiness.

    I wrote "The Wedding Poem," for my mom and step dad's wedding. It is a reminder that God needs to be first in any marriage. It's true that a couple who prays and seeks God together, will be more likely to have a stronger bond in their marriage. Their marriage will be built upon a good foundation and can last through many trials, to stand the test of time. Let us not forget that marriage was designed and ordained by God and finds its fulfillment in Him. Marriage is a gift from God that unites two bodies as one.

Dedicated to my mom and Ken.

Mark 10:8

Chad Joseph Thieman

Wedding on the Beach

(Alternate version, "Wedding by the Beach")

In a gazebo, by the beach they stand,
Two lovers hand in hand,
Looking intently into each others eyes,
Sharing their vows beneath a blue sky.

Each of them speaking words from the heart,
Making the promise, until death not to part.

A bond of love is being formed this day,
As these two bodies become as one,
On the edge of this seemingly endless sea,
Beneath the rays of a midday sun.

God, family, and friends are witnesses here,
Beholding this beautiful sight,
As these two souls join together in love,
And two hearts begin to unite.

They place their wedding bands,
Upon each others hands;
It's a beautiful sight to be seen.
Their love is forever represented here,
By these two encircling rings.

A reminder of the true circle of love,
Man, his wife, and God above.

Let them never forget this holy bond,
And Heavenly Father, remind them always,
To seek your love from beyond.

And now as they move forward from here,
Lord, I pray you will bless all of their plans,
As they leave behind this cherished moment in time,
And their two sets of footprints in the sand.

I wrote "Wedding on the Beach," for my dad's wedding. This is an alternate version of the poem, since they actually got married in a gazebo that overlooked Kure Beach. The words in this poem fitted perfectly, with the beauty of the ceremony.

Dedicated to my dad and Kathy, who were married at Fort Fisher.

Mark 10:7-9

The Christmas Collection

Come hither, come hither,
And pray the world sees.

Come hither, young children,
Sing songs of praise,
And songs of peace.

Colossians 3:16
James 5:13

It's a Lover's Christmas

It's a lover's Christmas,
Let's make angels in the snow,
After that we will go inside,
Beneath the mistletoe.

The fire burning on the hearth,
Will warm us through the night.
While stories of the infant's birth,
Are shared by candlelight.

If you celebrate the tradition of Christmas, then remember the Messiah and what He was born to do.

Dedicated to Erik and Crystal.

Matthew 1:18
Luke 2:1-20

New Year's in Perrysville

Part 1 - The Final Descent

The sun reflects thoughtfully, upon the frozen lake,
Where the children of Perrysville would gather to skate,
As if to ponder of the year it leaves behind,
And its final descent through that western gate.
For tomorrow at dawn, a new one it will find,
When from the east its rays again shine,
Over the rolling hills blanketed in white.
Until then it must wait through a long winter's night.

Part 2 - Another Year Passed

The houses in Perrysville give off a soft and warm glow.
The rooftops and sidewalks are all covered in snow.
New Year's Day is but only a few hours away,
And families gather together near the fireplace to pray,
Giving thanks for the blessings of another year passed,
And yet for another good year of favor they ask.
Outside, the white frosted village seems silent this eve,
While the townspeople in their dwellings wait and believe.

Part 3 - At The Village North End

There's an old stone church at the village north end,
And raised above houses, a clock that struck ten.
Two more with bell towers, a mile further down the road,
On the outskirts of town, by the old country store,
Where Mr. Smith sells produce on slanted tables of wood,
And his daughter Elizabeth does chores for him good.
Not long until midnight, soon the new year will be here,
And all the townspeople will gather with cheer.

Part 4 - This Midnight Hour

The moon from its perch, gives off a faint and soft glow.
The trees in the wood are all laden with snow.
The church bells in the distance, the only sound heard,
Through the cold winter air, they speak with no words.
Heralding in the new year, with various chimes,
These bells seem to dance to their musical rhymes.
For miles they are heard from their lofty church towers,
Proclaiming the strike of this midnight hour.

Part 5 - Make Merry

The moon and the stars watch from above,
As the townspeople scurry out of their homes,
Many of them without hat or glove,
Out into snow shoveled streets they come,
Some without shoes upon feet,
Toasting with New Years cheers and friendly greets.
But not too long, did the town folk tarry,
Only enough to laugh and make merry.

Part 6 - New Years

New Years in Perrysville came with a chill,
And the celebrations outside were shortened.
For the cold winter air drove the townspeople in,
And children danced by the fire with their closest of kin.
But before too long, they will all head to bed,
So as to awake in time to welcome the sun,
And its glorious spread, as it lifts above the horizon.
For with it will bring, the dawning of the new year.

Chad Joseph Thieman

Part 7 - The Sun's Great Arrival

Mr. Roberts was the first in town to awaken,
And he raised the flag, down at the old fire station.
But soon the whole town was bustling once again,
From the smallest child to the oldest of men.
All gathered outside for the sun's great arrival,
For this sight would not easily be rivaled.
As the sun peaked over the white-dressed hills,
Its rays brought some relief to the cold winter's chills.

Perrysville is named after Perrysburg, Ohio, where I was raised. I also drew some inspiration from the paintings of Kinkade and the small town of Blowing Rock, which is located in the heart of the Blue Ridge Mountains, in North Carolina.

Dedicated to Matt and Amanda.

Malachi 1:11

Snowy Winter Sleigh Ride

It is getting late and I have to go,
I wish I could remain here though,
But it's a seven mile ride in knee deep snow,
Beneath downy flake and naked bough.

I give these horse reins a whip and pull,
And glide forward through that fresh drifted snow.
There is no time to waste, I know.
It won't be long 'til the stars begin to show.

While in the wood all laden with snow,
I come upon a young deer, the smallest of doe,
Capering through the fresh fallen snow,
It seems to me, a most playful soul.

I don't have much time to reflect here though.
I must make haste,
Only three miles left to go!
And Old Man Winter's hands are growing ever so cold.

This poem was just for fun. I wanted to take the reader through a winter wonderland. "Snowy Winter Sleigh Ride," paints a beautiful scene of a sleigh ride through a refreshing winter scape. I have many fond memories of snowy winters as a child and look forward to making more of them, starting this winter, after I move to Asheville.

Dedicated to my friend Jeff and his family.

Psalm 147:16

The Christmas Candle

A flame proceeded forth from living fire.
And the Christmas candle was lit.

The first and greatest candlestick,
Through whom all other candles find,
A fire to share at Christmastime.

Yet was the candle lit on this day?
Nay!

And shall it burn but only for a day?
If this be true, then I shalt not stay,
I shalt not stay.

But what if it be a lie?
And every day be Christmastime.

And will our candle light remain,
If we refuse others the flame?

And how has the fire come to this wick?
That, merry gentlemen, I do not know,
This fire will burn in many though,
This fire will burn in many though.

*"The Christmas Candle," is a parable and analogy relating to Christ
and those who are born of God, through Christ. Several verses in scripture
seem to point to the idea that Christ was not born on Christmas morning.
Christmas was the day that ancient cultures celebrated the birthday of the
sun. True Christmas is when the Sun of Righteousness is born in the hearts
of men. The term Christmas refers to the body of Christ, and His sacrifice
that brought us eternal life.*

Malachi 4:2
John 8:12

The True Meaning of Christmas

The true meaning of Christmas is not what it seems.
It's not about candy canes or sugarplum dreams.
It's not about decorating the house with red and with greens.
It's not about Santa and reindeer or hand-painted nativity scenes.

Do you know what happens every year on Christmas morn'?
The sun lifts up higher and can represent Christ being born.
It moves up a notch in the sky, after three days of dread,
And can also remind us of Christ being raised from the dead.

Every Christmas the sun starts its cycle all over again.
The sun on this day is sometimes worshiped by men,
But still this is not the meaning of the word,
The meaning of Christmas has yet to be heard.

It's not about snowmen or presents beneath the tree.
It's not about leaving out cookies and hot minted teas.
It's not about shopping or children sitting on Santa's knee.
The true meaning of Christmas is so very easy to see.

Just look up the basic definition of "mass,"
And you'll know the true meaning of Christmas at last.
This term means unity within a body or form.
Christmas is the body of Christ, in which His spirit is born.

We should celebrate our Heavenly Father every day,
By coming together in Christ's Spirit and showing love's way.
For only after the Son arises within the hearts of all men,
Will we all be a part of true Christmas my friend.

Christmas is actually the birthday of the sun. So to me, true Christmas is when the Son is born within. Jesus never taught us to celebrate His birthday or to decorate a Christmas tree. He taught us to do the will of the Father and worship God in spirit and in truth. That is what really pleases Him, and we can do that by serving others and by giving praise and thanksgiving to God every single day.

Jeremiah 10:3-5
2 Corinthians 13:5

Chad Joseph Thieman

Proverbs by the Author:

A wise man attracts people with his wisdom, and holds them together with his love.

- Proverbs 24:5

No man can out give God, I dare you to try.

- Matthew 19:29, Luke 6:38, Luke 12:33

The people in your life who you despise the most, are probably the same people that need your love most of all.

- Matthew 5:43-48

How poor the rich man is, who seeks only to invest in his own livelihood and how rich the poor man, who invests all into others. Indeed the rich man is weighed down by his many possessions, but the poor man finds it easy to carry his load and receives everything he needs.

- Matthew 19:16-26

Some people have complex and burdensome religions, but mine is simple, bear the burdens of others.

- James 1:27

It is better for one to be a servant first, so that they may become a righteous king.

- Luke 16:9-13

Christ told us that whoever repents and believes in Him, would never die; therefore, those who are born of God, have become eternal spirits. Death for them is like casting off their garments and dancing in the pure essence of Christ.

- John 11:26, John 6:58, Philippians 1:21-26

When the earth bleeds from within, and the sea and rivers become as blood, and the birds and fish are covered in oil, then will humanity repent? Will we then turn and seek the face of the Lord, or will our hearts continue to be hardened and our minds continue to devise schemes?

- Revelation 8:8-9, Revelation 16:3-7

The Father is not in everyone. Even if a man had a single drop of living water within his vessel, he would not think or practice evil against his brother. The Father's Spirit must fill the temple of a man. Only one who is born of the Spirit through Christ, has the Father living within. These have become the children of God. We are not to worship the creation but rather the Creator, for even nature itself awaits the revealing of the sons of God.

- Romans 8:1-21, Ephesians 4:9-10

You are only one piece of a much larger puzzle. To see the big picture, we all need to come together in Christ.

- 1 Corinthians 12:12-27

A change of heart will change the world, and a seeker of truth, will become a harbor of understanding.

- 2 Chronicles 7:14-15, Jeremiah 5:1

Chad Joseph Thieman

Once love lives within you, then you can begin to plant the seeds of peace.

- 1 John 4:7-21

God will measure his mercy and love out to you, according to the mercy and love that you have measured out, to the least of His people.

- Mark 4:24, Luke 6:38

The Kingdom of Heaven is developing on earth and those who are of the world cannot comprehend it. The seed was planted, the crop is maturing, and the harvest is soon to come. When He who planted will come into His Kingdom and be satisfied.

- Colossians 1:13

There are no religions or denominations in the Kingdom of Heaven, for all are of one mind and partake of the same Spirit.

- James 1:27, Philippians 1:27

Once you are born of the Spirit, you have become a child of God, in Christ. Even if you were to break fellowship, the relationship would still stand. You have already given permission to the Father, to discipline you as His child. Our loving Father will always discipline His children when they stray, because it is through His discipline that He proves His love for us.

- Hebrews 12:6-8

Love and forgiveness are the only two gifts that I know for sure, benefit both the giver and the receiver.

- Luke 7:47

Christ is an offshoot of the Father, much like a branch is an offshoot of a tree. Christ is in the Father, a part of the Father, and one with the Father.

- John 17:2-5

Come down to the river, to wash your sins away, and partake at the table, learning of the faith. Put the desires of your flesh to death every day, and continue to live in a spiritual way.

- Luke 3:2-4, Luke 22:14-20

We have freedom in Christ, so why join with those who would make us slaves once again? We are no longer slaves but are free to bear good fruit and reap the benefits of the Spirit. The Spirit alone defines us. Whomever seeks truth from the Spirit of God, will find his freedom, but he who seeks after the traditions and doctrines of men, will be enslaved by them.

- Galatians 2:4

Quit living in your reality and seek out that higher reality, the reality of the Kingdom of Christ. To enter this reality you must be born again, not by flesh but by God's Spirit. Our fight is in the spiritual realm, not in the physical. The Kingdom of Heaven is the true reality of life, and we need to be watchful that others don't confuse us, and pull us down into their reality and worldview of death. Instead we who are spirit born and matured in the knowledge and understanding of God, must with faith bring others into our reality of life.

- Ephesians 6:12

Some invest their treasures in others, some their time, and some their talents; but the greatest investment you can make, is one of Spirit and of love.

- 1 Corinthians 3:6-11

When you have seen the result of your work and know that you have indeed helped others, don't let it leaven the bread within you, for love is never puffed up.

- 1 Corinthians 13:4

Christ is not the only king in the Kingdom of Heaven. If this were true, then He would not hold the title, "King of kings."

- Revelation 17:14

We all have our purpose here and though we have differences, one day they will dissolve, when mankind realizes that there is something greater at work here, after the Son arises within us all.

- 1 Corinthians 15:22, 1 Timothy 4:10

The Kingdom and Family of God

God is a family of spirit. The Holy Spirit conceived the Son and can pray to the Father on our behalf. The Father is the only Godhead. Christ is of the Father and represents the Father on earth, just as believers are of His Holy Spirit and represent His wife and bride. All spirits in the Spirit family submit to the Father. The Father is one. All spirits that are born of God, proceed from the Father and have their place in Him. Just as those in the flesh came from Adam and through Eve, so too has the Son of God come from the Father and through the Holy Spirit. Christ, Himself has stated that the Father is the only true God, meaning that the Father is in all of His spirit children, and they are all in Him. Jesus Christ, the firstborn of all spirit children, is not ashamed to call us His brothers and sisters. He is the only begotten of the Father, and we in turn are all begotten through Him. He is the vine and we are His branches.

The Son of God is not the same as the Father. He left the Godhead in the beginning and willingly took on a separate identity from the Father. The Father is the one and only true God, as Christ and Paul both clearly stated and testified of throughout Scripture. The Father is in all who have been born of Him through Christ. The Son of God and those who are sons through Him, listen and are taught from the Father who is the source of all wisdom, knowledge, and understanding. The Son has chosen to remain in submission to the Father and reign through man. The Father is the only Godhead and the entirety of God. Scripture clearly tells us that the Father is the head of Christ, and Christ is the head of His church. Christ has been exalted higher than all the rest of creation, but He is always subordinate to the Father, just as our spirits always remain subordinate to Christ, even though all spirits in this Spirit family are of God and a part of Him. Spirit gives birth to spirit and spirit must submit to Spirit, but there is only one God, our Father. The Father alone is the fullness and the head of this Spirit family. Christ will hand all things back over to the Father, after all things are brought under His authority and are united with God. Then the Father will become all in all.

- John 17:3, 1 Corinthians 8:6

Parables by the Author

The Sun of Wisdom Parable

Wisdom is a rising sun. In this age of darkness, its light has been hidden, but soon it will shine bright and lovely again, when the morning has come. Once this sun arises, all men will be filled with understanding, and never will its light be hidden from them again, for this sun shall never set.

- Ecclesiastes 2:13

The Sunflower Parable

The Kingdom of Heaven is like a single sunflower, which was planted in a large field. When it died, a strong wind came and scattered about its seed. Much of the seed took root, and soon the field was filled with bright yellow sunflowers. If only all the new sunflowers understood how to invest their seed, then what a marvelous site we would be!

- Matthew 13:24

The Fisherman Parable

Whatever you cast out you will receive back to yourself, and you may even catch an increase. So cast out faith, hope, love, peace, and lots and lots of happiness. Don't cast out negativity or anger because you may catch a monstrous fish, which could swallow you whole.

- Luke 5:5-7
- Matthew 13:47-48

The Parable of the Rising Sun

As the sun is reborn every morning, so to are we to be reborn and filled with the living Spirit of love. The day star must arise within our hearts and shine forth as the sun in the heavens, who's light reaches from one end of the earth to the other. We are to be a light to the world, so that the fullness of the Kingdom can be realized. We are to be the suns of the morning, the suns of the harvest. True change only comes through the Spirit of God, which must first take up residence within the hearts of men. When the Spirit comes down and enters into its temple, it is as if the sun itself has entered within the man. The light therein, shines forth upon other temples and many others are also filled with its light.

A sun must arise within,
The day star shining ever bright,
Dawning in the hearts of men,
A sun of eternal life.

- 2 Peter 1:19

The Parable of the Candle

Love is like a flame burning brightly on the wick of a large candle. When the flame touches the wicks of other candles, they too are set on fire. Each has an individual flame and yet all received their fire from the first candle, therefore, they are all still a part of the original flame. Even if your candle has but a small flame, still it can light others and set the world ablaze.

- Psalm 18:28
- Luke 8:16

The Inner Tree Parable

A seed of love must be planted within you. This seed must be watered by living water, so that it will grow up and flourish within and bear good fruit to others, which contain within them, more seeds of love.

- Proverbs 11:30

Chad Joseph Thieman

The Tree of Life Parable

A mustard seed was planted in the ground and grew up into a large tree, watered by living water. This water enters first into the root and travels up through the trunk of the tree, giving life to all its branches. My friends, do not the larger branches of a tree sprout forth and support all the smaller branches? Are not the larger branches more important than the smaller ones? Therefore, become large branches and sprout forth and tend to the smaller ones that you may bear much fruit, and be among the greatest in the Kingdom of Heaven. Remember, the larger branches of a tree will not always see the glory of the fruit but rather they support all the smaller ones who see it. The larger branches indeed accept the greater burden, but their glory is to uphold all the smaller branches. In this way those who are least among you are the greatest and the greatest must make himself least of all. Both the church and the Kingdom should be set up in such a way that spirit willingly submits to spirit, with everyone seeking his or her proper place within the tree of Christ. Some are greater branches and some are lesser, but the tree must work together as one to produce the fruit. Know who is greater and who is lesser than you, in the Kingdom of Heaven. Remember, the sower is greater than the seed, yet he tends to it, until it is full grown. Now, all who believe in the Father and Son, have become branches of Christ. The one who rejects a branch of Christ, has rejected Christ, Himself. The tree stands as one, and all the branches must bear good fruit or else they will be cut off.

- Matthew 23:9-11
- Revelation 22:16

The Holy Grail Parable

Which was made for the other? Was water created for the chalice, or was the chalice made to hold the water? The body is a temple of the Spirit, and the fullness of God dwelt within Christ. Therefore, all who are filled with the Father's Spirit, have become a holy grail and their water runneth over.

- Psalm 23:5-6

The Fountain of Life Parable

The Father's Spirit is living water that flows through all believers, giving them life. We must become fountains of this life giving water, so that others may also drink from the wellspring of Christ. His love is an endless well, and we are to pour forth its water, until all have received of it and are satisfied.

The Father is like an ocean of Spirit,
Flowing through the inlet of Christ,
Filling up those dried up river beds,
Believers filled with the water of life.

- Song of Solomon 4:15
- Psalm 36:9

The Parable of the Harvest

Even fools plant in the earth, but a wise man plants in Heaven. Do you not understand that your harvest is your reward? Whatever a man sows, whether it be of the earth or of the Spirit that the man shall reap. If you don't plant anything, then you will reap nothing, but if you sow much seed, then you will be great in the Kingdom of Heaven. Only a foolish farmer expects a harvest without first planting his seed. If you hold on to a seed, then all you will have in the end is the seed but if you plant, water, and nurture it, then you will reap a great harvest.

At first you will not see the fruit of your labor. Be patient, wait a season, and you will see it. Remember that the type of seed you plant, the amount of light, and the water it receives, as well as the quality of the soil it is planted in, all factor in. All of these things help determine the harvest that you will receive. Ask the Father for His Spirit, so that you may plant only good seed.

Every day you have the opportunity to plant into the lives of others. Every missed opportunity is another seed that goes unplanted. Everything you possess is a possible seed that you can invest, so look for the perfect time to invest them into the Kingdom. Yes, even you are a seed to be planted.

Now when you plant a seed, you don't use a stick of dynamite to blow a hole in the ground, rather, you remove a little bit of dirt and plant it gently.

Once the seed has taken root, then it will grow up, mature, and understand the greater things.

The one who plants is greater than that which is planted but for now tend to your harvest. For the greatest among you must show yourselves as the least of all. Now if a farmer plants seed in his field, how is he repaid? Is he not sustained by his harvest? Whatever he sows will grow up, mature, and sustain him. If a man sows, shall he not also reap, from that which was sown? Let each man be sustained by his own harvest, the fruit of his labor shall sustain him.

Shall one eat from another man's harvest? No, by ones own field, shall a man eat. It would not be right for a man to do the labor, and not eat of the fruit of that labor. In the scriptures Paul said that since he had planted spiritual seed, he was entitled to a material harvest; however, he did not boast of this or claim such a right for the sake of the Kingdom. I say that whatever spiritual seed one plants, it will mature and grow up, and remember the one who planted it. This is how the farmer is sustained, by his harvest. All who plant good seed, their spiritual and physical needs should be met. Those who teach the Gospel of the Kingdom of God, should be sustained by it.

Planting seed and investing in the lives of others, can bring forth a great harvest for both parties. Do your giving in secret, and let God water your investment and bring it to fruition. Do not think that investing in others is loss. When you invest in others with love, you invest in the Kingdom of Heaven and the better the soil, the better the harvest. My friends, always look for good soil before planting your seed. If you wish to make your harvest even greater, then when you first start seeing your harvest spring up, invest the very first fruits of your harvest, back into the Kingdom. When your harvest has come in fullness, you will know it has come; thresh and winnow the wheat, and separate the chaff from the grain.

- *Mark 4:26-27*
- *1 Corinthians 9:11-14*
- *Galatians 6:8-10*

The Parable of the Wind

Love is like a light breeze or a peaceful and gentle wind. You cannot see it, but you know that it's there. You can feel it in that quiet place, you can hear it when you calm your soul, you can see the effects it has on others, and how it guides and moves us still.

- John 3:8

The Living Bible Parable

Christ said that He was the Amen, and we know from Scripture that the Old Test-Ament represents physical Israel, while the New Test-Ament are Spirit filled believers. The heavenly Amen will come again for His bride and consort, Ament. We are called to be living Bibles, with God's Word written upon the pages of our hearts. We must stand as a testimony of Christ and His cross, and become living epistles opened up for all to read.

- 2 Corinthians 3:1-6

The Fruit and Seed Parable

If someone gave you a piece of fruit and you ate it, the fruit would only satisfy you for a couple hours and you would be hungry once again. However, if someone gave you a piece of fruit and you planted the seeds that were within it, then you would reap several trees full of fruit. Good deeds done in Love for another person, are like good fruit filled with the seeds of love.

- 2 Corinthians 9:9-11

The Body of Christ Parable

All true believers are one in Christ. Each plays the role of a member of this larger body. If the body is going to function properly, then all of its members must work together. Brothers and sisters, let each one of you perform his or her own function within the body, according to his or her own God-given talents, knowledge, and gifts. In the world people achieve success on their own, but it is not to be so, for you who are in Christ. The believer can only find true success, by carrying out their role in the body and by working together with other members of the body.

- 1 Corinthians 12

The Blazing Love Parable

Every single time that you give cheerfully, you overcome the world. So give to others in the Spirit of love, and then love will spread like a wildfire across the earth. Look for those in need and supply their needs happily. Invest in others every chance you get, and it won't be long before complete strangers will start to invest in you. Love travels fast and sets the world on fire. So spread your flame until the entire earth is set ablaze.

- 2 Corinthians 9:10

The Parable of the Two Grape Vines

In the midst of a vineyard, stood two grape vines. One produced the most excellent grapes, while the other was beginning to wither and rot. The vine-dresser pulls up the rotting vine and throws its rotten fruit into the wine press of wrath. He then prunes the branches on the fruitful vine, so that it may produce even more fruit. The branches were the means, for each vine to bring forth its fruit. The branches of the rotting vine brought forth rotten fruit, but the branches of the fruitful vine brought forth good fruit. Every branch that did not bring forth good fruit, was cut off and thrown away.

- John 15:1-8

The Parable of the Weary Farmer

There is a farmer who has been planting his seed, season after season, waiting for his harvest to come. Though the rain falls and the sun shines, he has yet to see the fruit of his labor. The soil in which most of his seed was planted, was not good soil. Therefore, pray that this farmer finds good soil that he may finally see an abundant harvest.

- Matthew 13:1-9

The Thirsty Tree Parable

Humanity is like a thirsty tree receiving living water, now that the Spirit of love is entering in through the roots.

- Jeremiah 17:7-8

The Gospel of the Kingdom of God

God created the angels before man, but a third of the angels who were under Lucifer's rule, all rebelled with him. They attempted to take Heaven by storm. God knew the only sure way to have beings who would remain obedient, was to reproduce His Spirit. Those who are born of God are greater than the angels, who are only as messengers and servants of the King. Those born of God are sons and daughters. Only a son or daughter can be an heir of a kingdom; therefore, unless you are born again, you cannot inherit the Kingdom of God. Flesh and blood can by no means inherit it.

Those who are born of God cannot sin or die, for there is no sin or death in Christ and His seed remains in Him. You must become a new creation in Christ. Christ died so we could live forever. That is the good news of the Gospel. Christ said that whoever repents and believes in Him, will never die. God will purify, transform, and adopt your physical body. He will make you a temple of His righteousness, but your spirit must first be born of God. One born of God will never die because they are born of Spirit, not of the flesh but of God. These are fruitful branches in the tree of Christ. Any branch that does not produce good fruit will be broken off and thrown away. Spirit gives birth to spirit, and only by sowing the spirit, can one reap of the Spirit. This is how one becomes a part of the Family of God and the greatest in the Kingdom of God.

When you accept the sacrifice that Christ made for the remission of sins, believe that He is risen and ascended to His Father, and seek out the Father in true repentance through Christ; then, and only then, will you be able to receive true life. Be baptized in the name of our Lord Jesus Christ and you will be filled with the Holy Spirit. As a child in the family of God, you are at once put under the authority of the church. You are to be placed under those who will train you up in the knowledge of God. Only after maturing, and becoming one in mind with Christ and His Father, will you be given responsibility over the Kingdom. Just as the Father was present in Christ and Christ in His Father, so too is Christ to be present within you and you in Him. All will be as one in the Father and Son.

Christ is the Tree of Life and believers are the branches of this tree. The Kingdom of God is developing on the earth, it is unseen to the world, and it will come into its fullness when Christ returns into His kingdom. Go forth and spread the good news of the Kingdom of God. Baptize and make disciples of all the nations. Go and proclaim the Gospel of the Kingdom of God, and reserve the secret teachings (the hidden wisdom in the parables), for those who have matured in Christ. This is the Gospel of our Lord.

Even if I stand alone and everyone else forsakes me, still I will stand for the truth of love that has saved me. I am not ashamed of the Gospel, for it has been misunderstood. - Chad

Hebrews 1:3-6

A Note From the Author

First I would like to thank you for the purchase of this book. It is my hope that this collection of poetry will inspire you in many different ways. My life is now an open book for all to read. This is my life's work, and I have faith that the Heavenly Father has inspired much of what is written within these pages. I am only an instrument, a mere writer of simple poetry. It is my Father in Heaven, who is the true poet in me. I write to inspire others, to plant these words into their lives, and to promote my Heavenly Father above all in my life. There are far too many today, who are trying to gain success apart from the Father. So the message I would like to leave you with is this: true success only comes from above my friend. We are to be temples filled up with the Spirit of love. So use your talents to glorify the Father. Always invest in others and promote the Heavenly Father above all, then God's Spirit will move, and He will cause others to invest in and promote you. It only takes one random act of kindness to trigger a domino effect of love. We all have thousands of opportunities every single day to transform lives.

Remember that Christ told us to seek the Kingdom of Heaven first of all, and then everything else would be handed to us freely and poured out into our laps. Therefore, the Kingdom of Heaven has to be attainable right here and right now. It is a way of viewing the world, yourself, and the people around you differently. It is a new attitude, a change of heart, a higher reality, and a new way of living, which completely reverses one's way of thinking. It is seeing everyone and everything in a new light, as an opportunity and an investment. Once you have developed this way of seeing, then you can participate in the Kingdom of Heaven around you. You can plant what is needed in each life and accept what is given freely from others. Christ told us to seek the Kingdom like a little child, and that if you continue to seek it, you will indeed find it. I tell you the truth, the Kingdom of Heaven is among, within, and around those who believe. They just need their Jesus glasses to see it. When you look at the world through His perception, you realize the truth is Christ, and you see that the proof is right in front of your eyes and has always been there in front of you.

When Christ returns, He will come into His kingdom. His kingdom is here, and it is developing, and it is yet to come into the fullness of glory. Christ is the sower and the mustard seed of the Kingdom of Heaven. He sowed His body, His spirit, and His life. His kingdom is a kingdom that is rising in the midst of many kingdoms. It is not a physical kingdom, but rather, a spiritual one. It is the light that will fill and consume the hearts of men, as a sun begins to rise within. Terror, fear, suffering, and darkness are trying hard to stand their ground and bring forth the false light, but the false light is not the same as the true light. The true light comes from the Father above. The enemies of our God will not be able to stand against the light of His coming. Look now and see the Spirit of God rising within the hearts of men. Ask for the Father's Holy Spirit to be poured out upon you and to fill you within. Surrender to the Potter, and let the Spirit of Christ possess you. He is the vine, and you are called to be a branch of Him. Soon you will begin on a new adventure and start writing your Kingdom story. Peace be with you my friends, and may the light of Christ arise within your hearts that you may also go forth and leave your mark.

For this book to be a success, I know that God's Spirit must move through the hearts of those who read these words. I know with great confidence that it will, and I hope that you will see the opportunity to get this book into the hands of today's youth because they will be tomorrow's leaders. Those who can help me, are those who don't have to ask me what kind of help I need; rather, they know how to help and put everything into doing it. There are bookstores, libraries, and churches that could use this book to reach and save many souls. Most of the marketing done for this book is going to be through the moving of God's Spirit. Remember that we are to share the good news of the Gospel of life. I feel called to proclaim the Gospel of Christ, but many have forgotten me, lost interest in me, or ignored me because of my faith; but to you who have remembered me, pray for me, always. I am only a single candle looking for those to share a flame. This is only the beginning of my Kingdom story, to the Father be all the Honor and Glory!

We are not to build on any other foundation, then the one that has already been laid out for us. For the foundation of the Kingdom of Heaven is good and strong, and will not be shaken from its place. - Chad

1 Corinthians 3:10-15

An Invitation to Forgiveness

This is an invitation to forgiveness. I would like to invite each of you to ask for the forgiveness of your sins, to our Heavenly Father and our Lord Jesus Christ. Repentance is not simply saying that you are sorry, true repentance is seeking mercy from God, promising a change, and acting on that promise to change your way of life. A lifestyle change takes determination, as well as a change of attitude and state of mind. You must understand that you cannot overcome temptation apart from God. Since this is true, there needs to be a relationship and communion of Spirit. Those who believe on Christ are no longer under the law; therefore, we are no longer called to follow a set of rules. We are called to have a relationship with the Father and the Son. We are called into the oneness of the Spirit. Through this relationship we see our error and seek to do the will of our Father, over the will and desires of our flesh.

All of your sins will be forgiven, if you seek to do the will of the Father in Heaven. So come to Him with an honest, humble, and contrite heart, in mourning and fasting, in fear and trembling; then He will see your brokenness, and forgive you of all your sin. Sins are forgiven primarily through Christ's sacrifice which paid the debt for our sin, but also by obeying and serving the Father in faithfulness, and by bringing others into the Kingdom of Heaven. Christ is the one who washes us clean through His blood, and we must go to the Father through Christ. If you return to God and begin to do the will of the Father, then you will be washed by the blood of the Lamb and be cleansed of all unrighteousness. It is by His blood that we are made white as snow and through His Spirit we find salvation for our souls. All who believe on Christ and truly seek forgiveness from the Father, are forgiven. There is no room left for guilt in your life; there is no room left for fear. Perfect love casts out all fear, and you are a precious child in the sight of the Father.

Joel 2:12-13, Matthew 3:10-12, Matthew 4:12-17, Acts 26:20-21

Chad Joseph Thieman

About the Author

As a young child, Chad Thieman grew up in Northwest Ohio. He attended Catholic schools and churches, and then later attended public schools. His family moved to North Carolina in the foothills of the Blue Ridge Mountains when he was in his first year of high school. It would be in North Carolina where he would obtain his inspiration to write Christian poetry. One of his foremost inspirations came while reading the popular poem, *"Footprints in the Sand"* by Mary Stevenson. The first poem Chad wrote was titled *"The Crosses,"* which was actually a short story inspired by Stevenson's poem. He was also moved by the scenic mountains around him, and found in those mountains the comfort of the Lord. His compassionate poems have been such a comfort to both his family and friends, that he feels compelled to continue to motivate, inspire, and encourage others.

Chad's enthusiasm for poetry has continued for over the past fifteen years. He has compiled and written an anthology of 101 inspirational poems in his first book, *"101 Treasurable Poems of Faith, Hope, and Love."* As a follow up to his book, Chad plans on publishing a coastal poetry collection book entitled, *"Sea of Serenity,"* with photography, which has always been his second love. His faith has always been a simple faith and has been the driving force behind most of his work. His religion is love and service. He believes wholeheartedly that much of his work has been inspired by God, and he prays that his poetry will have a positive impact on the lives of his readers.

A Tribute

This bonus poetry section is a tribute from my family to a wonderful lady, our loving grandmother, Dorothy A. Boyd.

Grandma, we wish you were here to see our accomplishments; We hope that you can somehow. We hope that you know how much you are missed and so very well loved. We pray that God will hold you forever in His arms, until you are called forth from the grave on Resurrection Day. Then we will get to see you face to face once again and share in a most beautiful and glorious reunion.

The Pillow

Written by Debra S. Moore

Here is a pillow
to lay down your head,
while you rest in the evenings
before going to bed.

There's something magical
beyond its cotton and lace.
Resting with it takes you back
to a special time and place.

It's not just a pillow,
for if you look closely you'll see.
It is made out of something
you once made for me.

The cotton has yellowed
and doesn't quite look its best,
but it did years ago
as a slip under my dress.

You sewed it with love,
I remember that day.
That's why I've kept it for years
and haven't thrown it away.

The slip was a keepsake.
It reminded me of so much.
How you've taught me to give
and how truly to love.

I could never bring myself
to take it all apart,
unless, it was made into something,
for someone dearest to my heart.

So this pillow is for you, Grandma.
Look even closer and you'll see,
that it's made out of the same love,
as when you made it for me.

Fingerprints on Our Hearts

The Lord has called you away from here,
And we will miss you so.
The time has come for you to leave this place,
And to our Father you must go.

You left an imprint on our lives,
And it's so hard for us to say good-bye,
But for awhile we must part.

We will never forget you, Grandma.
You left your fingerprints on our hearts.

We pray our Father will hold you forever,
And now your spirit is finally free.
Soon we will be called home to Heaven,
And with you, forever we will be.

You left an imprint on our lives.
And it's so hard for us to say good-bye,
But for awhile we must part.

We will always remember you, Grandma.
You left your fingerprints on our hearts.

Written By: Chad Joseph Thieman

A Tribute to

Dorothy A. Boyd

March 25, 1920 - April 16, 2007

It was some years ago that the Lord called you.
He softly whispered your name.
How we wanted you to stay,
But in Heaven there is no pain.

We miss you each and every day.
Cherished memories fill our hearts.
We'll keep you in our thoughts and prayers,
as long as we're apart.

You filled our lives with love and laughter,
Which made us who we are.
You loved us unconditionally.
Living without you has been so hard.

One day we'll be together again,
What a heavenly reunion that will be,
To embrace you and see your smile,
Throughout all eternity.

We love and miss you so very much,
        Your Family,

Written by Debra S. Moore

Index

Chad Joseph Thieman

Special Acknowledgments

Curtis Neil - Investment Partner and Promotional Manager

I met my investment partner/promotional manager working at the Blockade-Runner Beach Resort, at Wrightsville Beach. We worked together for nearly two years. Curtis is a wonderful, God fearing man, and I am thankful for being his friend. Curtis has been a help in many different ways; not only did he help me get copyrights, find a publisher, promote my work, and invest in my book, but he has also helped me to stay on track and spiritually grounded. Thank you Curtis for all your help and support, past, present, and future.

Kim Brandt - Proofreader and Editor

I owe Kim credit for proofreading my work. For the most part I listened to her advice that is when it didn't interfere with the flow, rhyme, or message of the poem.

Jonathan Mull - Foreword

Jonathan is a good friend of mine, who I have known now for several years. I always give him a hard time about becoming a preacher. I still think God is going to take him down that path. I hope to stand beside him one day, while he preaches the message of the Kingdom to the people.

Jillian Smith - Back Cover Photo

My good friend Jillian, took the photo of Curtis and I, while we were all still working together at the Blockade-Runner. I really appreciate you taking the picture for us Jillian, it turned out really well.

Jamie Cornett DeSantis - Proofreader

After making several changes to my book, I called upon my friend Jamie to go through and help me find any punctuation errors. She was also a big help to me in the proofreading process. Thank you Jamie!

Larry Thieman - Cover Photo

My dad took the cover photo. We took a day trip a few years back to High Shoals Falls, in South Mountain State Park. This beautiful waterfall symbolizes to me, how the Spirit of God flows down upon us and shows the peacefulness and beauty found in God's creation. Good photography Dad!

Debbi Moore - About the Author & 2 Tribute Poems

My mom wrote the "About the Author" section and contributed two of her own poems as a tribute to my grandmother, who this book is dedicated to. Thank you Mom for your kind words.

Chad Thieman - Front and Back Cover Design and Background Photos.

I graduated from Mcdowell Tech. in Marion, NC, with a degree in Advertising and Graphic Design. A special thank you to my graphic design and photography instructors.

May the latter rain pour down upon you,
and may the love of Christ fill you up, until your cup is overflowing.
You shall become like grass that never withers,
your days shall be without number. - Chad

James 5:7-8

All feedback can be sent to the author on his Facebook page.
Chad Joseph Thieman (Poetry Page)

Author's Website: inspiremepoetry.com

This book is available on amazon.com, barnesandnoble.com, booksamillion.com and at the author's website.

All poetry in this book may be shared, copied, and passed around, as long as reference is given to either the author or the book, and there is no profit made. If you wish to use the poetry in this book to raise money for a charity, you may contact the author at his website or Facebook page for permission to do so.

Upcoming books:

Sea of Serenity
- A collection of coastal poetry and photography.

101 Treasurable Poems of Life, Love, and Light
- An anthology of poetry, proverbs, and parables.

CPSIA information can be obtained
at www.ICGtesting.com
Printed in the USA
FFOW02n0640220316
22525FF